most current ed.

Frederick J. Augustyn Jr.

Dictionary of Toys and Games in American Popular Culture

Pre-publication REVIEWS, COMMENTARIES, EVALUATIONS . . .

"Collectors, researchers, and those who simply love toys will find *Dictionary of Toys and Games in American Popular Culture* an invaluable tool. The text brings the toys to life, describing them in both physical and cultural terms.

A good reference should be hard to put down and this one certainly is as the reader becomes reacquainted with favorite toys and learns fascinating tidbits about the culture surrounding them. Who would have thought that J. Edgar Hoover hung his paint-by-numbers canvases in the West Wing?"

Felicia F. Campbell, PhD
Editor, *Popular Culture Review*

"Centered on 1950s and 60s social and cultural history, the dictionary reaches back to the historical roots of many toys and games in the 1870s and forward to the present day. The geographic focus falls on the United States with some references to Europe and Asia. Several entries in the bulk of the dictionary explain the interaction among consumers, inventors, and manufacturers in addressing changing gender roles and emerging racial equality. This book closes with a fascinating 'Who's Who' of toy and game inventors, manufacturers, and distributors along with a useful bibliography.

This book would prove useful not only to collectors and nostalgic baby boomers but also to American social and cultural history students. In fact, a creative teacher could use it as a supplementary text in a 1950s/1960s class. Students and avid collectors could use the extensive bibliography to search for more detail on a particular toy or game."

Lauren Ann Kattner, PhD
Independent Scholar,
National Coalition
of Independent Scholars

More pre-publication
REVIEWS, COMMENTARIES, EVALUATIONS . . .

"From action figures to yo-yos, Augustyn has done Herculean work in compiling this *Dictionary of Toys and Games in American Popular Culture*. It is extremely comprehensive in nature, providing valuable information. Augustyn has utilized the dictionary format to include not just single objects but concepts and categories as well. For example, he titles one entry 'battery-operated toys' and another 'toys in movies.' In his accounting of games, he recounts the playing instructions and a history of the game along with the description. This is quite valuable as board games are a very distinct way to look at American culture and childhood. He places the toys and games in a historical context, suggesting how they have affected American culture. Curators and collectors will find the entries useful. This book is truly a trip down memory lane for baby boomers who will find themselves saying as they peruse the pages, 'I had one of those!'"

Sharon Smith, MA
Bascom Curator,
Missouri Historical Society,
Curator of Toy and Other Collections

~⟨≈⟩~

"In *Dictionary of Toys and Games in American Popular Culture*, Augustyn has filled a gap in the available literature on toys and games. While numerous guides for the serious collector abound, and smart-looking coffee-table books on

vintage toys are snatched up by nostalgic baby boomers, there has been a dearth of comprehensive, descriptive material on the subject. Augustyn's dictionary will be useful and interesting to a wide audience: collectors, trivia buffs, researchers and writers, and the simply nostalgic. The author places toys in their cultural, historical, and sometimes pedagogical perspectives, providing detailed descriptions of both generic categories and specific products. Augustyn's detailed visual descriptions jar the reader into vivid recollection of toys and games past, and provide several 'oh, yeah!' moments. This book is exceedingly well researched, with an extensive bibliography for those who want to explore the topic further."

Rochelle Hartman, MSLIS
Contributing Editor, *Public Libraries*;
Public Services Librarian,
Bloomington Public Library, Illinois

~⟨≈⟩~

"Toys and games reflect values and pass those values along to children; for this reason, it makes sense to study them carefully. This dictionary rewards the hunger for nostalgia as well as an academic interest. With entries including Frisbee and Mr. Potato Head, these small joys of study are communicated with energy and excitement. This book is recommended for libraries which serve the general public and scholars."

Peter C. Rollins, PhD
Editor-in-Chief, *Film & History:
An Interdisciplinary Journal
of Film and TV Studies*

The Haworth Reference Press
An Imprint of The Haworth Press, Inc.
New York • London • Oxford

NOTES FOR PROFESSIONAL LIBRARIANS AND LIBRARY USERS

This is an original book title published by The Haworth Reference Press, an imprint of The Haworth Press, Inc. Unless otherwise noted in specific chapters with attribution, materials in this book have not been previously published elsewhere in any format or language.

CONSERVATION AND PRESERVATION NOTES

All books published by The Haworth Press, Inc. and its imprints are printed on certified pH neutral, acid free book grade paper. This paper meets the minimum requirements of American National Standard for Information Sciences-Permanence of Paper for Printed Material, ANSI Z39.48-1984.

Dictionary of Toys and Games in American Popular Culture

THE HAWORTH PRESS

Contemporary Sports Issues
Frank Hoffmann, PhD, MLS
Martin Manning
Senior Editors

Dictionary of Toys and Games in American Popular Culture

Frederick J. Augustyn Jr.

The Haworth Reference Press
An Imprint of The Haworth Press, Inc.
New York • London • Oxford

Published by

The Haworth Reference Press, an imprint of The Haworth Press, Inc., 10 Alice Street, Binghamton, NY 13904-1580.

Cover design by Marylouise E. Doyle.

Library of Congress Cataloging-in-Publication Data

Augustyn, Frederick J.
    Dictionary of toys and games in American popular culture / Frederick J. Augustyn, Jr.
        p. cm.
    Includes bibliographical references (p.   ).
    ISBN 0-7890-1503-X (hard : alk. paper)—ISBN 0-7890-1504-8 (soft : alk. paper)
    1. Toys—United States—Dictionaries. 2. Games—United States—Dictionaries. I. Title.
NK9509.65.U6A95 2004
790.1'3—dc22
                                                                                    2003016133

ABOUT THE AUTHOR

Frederick J. Augustyn Jr., PhD, has been a librarian at the Library of Congress, in Washington, DC, since 1984 and is currently a cataloger in the Library's Social Sciences Cataloging Division. He has also worked as an archivist for the National Education Association in Washington, DC, and is a Smithsonian Docent at the National Museum of American History, also in Washington, DC. Dr. Augustyn has been a contributor to *Biographical Dictionary of American Sports, Statesmen Who Changed the World: A Bio-Bibliographical Dictionary of Diplomacy,* and *Political Parties & Elections in the United States: An Encyclopedia.*

CONTENTS

Instead of the old saw: "All is vanity," the more positive conclusion forces itself upon us that "all is play."

Johan Huizinga,
Homo Ludens: A Study of the Play Element in Culture

Introduction

Toys, in particular dolls and electric trains, are among the most popular collectibles in the United States. In addition to their desirability among hobbyists, toys shed light on society's changing attitudes toward childhood. They are mirrors of the fads and fashions of culture at large. Accordingly, a reference book on playthings can assist those interested in charting the development of popular culture as well as apprise collectors about the facts concerning some of their favorites. Although originally intended to amuse children, toys hold a fascination for adults. They intrigue those seeking to relive their childhoods, those attempting to re-create a youthful age that they think was too bereft of such cultural objects, and those pursuing a serious study of the social attitudes of earlier times. Many collectors, when remembering a bauble that evokes an earlier era, recognize that their grandparents had it, their parents probably threw it away, and it is now up to them to buy it back. The memory jogs that this book provides are a part of that recognition process.

At first homemade, as most household objects were, usually of wood, straw, or cloth, by the nineteenth century toys bore the imprint of the machine age. They were soon composed of the material of industry—metal—and later plastic. Gender-specific roles defined the world of childhood as they did society as a whole. Building toys for boys became particularly popular during the industrial age and less so during the service industry era when fantasy diversions gained prominence. But even during the early twentieth century, gender-neutral objects such as teddy bears and puppets appealed to both sexes. Popular usage indicated what market research later bore out—that the nonviolent action toys (such as trains and cars) purportedly only for young males had an attraction that included young women as well. In the later part of that century, dolls in male guise (or "action figures") such as G.I. Joe and *Star Wars* characters became desirable.

During the post–World War II accelerated consumer culture years, as the middle class in the United States expanded (and the baby boom marked a noticeable increase in children being born) the accumula-

1

tion of multiple playthings by both boys and girls arguably became a hallmark of the democratization of society. Expendable income increased and commercial toy makers rose to the challenge to fulfill consumers' desires. Toys have had a long history of commercial tie-ins almost since the time that they were first mass produced, although commercialization seemed more marked during these years. In the early twenty-first century, real-life hero figures such as firefighters and police officers truly arrived. A more open convergence of gender roles has recently occurred with Barbie, initially a fashion doll, going into previously largely male professions such as that of dentist and astronaut.

This book includes toys appearing as premiums with purchased products dispensed as promotional keepsakes at fast-food restaurants, often tied to the release of animated films. It addresses those objects distributed most often during the 1920s through the 1950s by way of mailing in cereal box tops. It also includes the depiction of toys in other popular culture forums, such as in films and on television. Rather than list manufacturers of particular products by the score, this book discusses a limited number of prominent or representative firms and expounds upon them, setting them in a cultural context.

In a one-volume reference book of this nature it is not possible to provide a photograph or drawing of every item mentioned. Consequently, instead of using a limited number of illustrations, excluding some toys and including others, a textual form of "audio description" of the objects, a technique increasingly employed by museum docents, is preferred. In use since the early 1980s, audio description seeks to make the visual aural by describing to visitors as thoroughly and consistently as possible the characteristics of and differences in objects. Originally, this was meant primarily to assist the visually impaired. But when these deep descriptions are translated into text, as in video documentaries that are close-captioned, the results are similar to intentionally detailed dictionary entries. Addressing the size, color, material composition, and designated age groups are part of the procedure.

This book does not presume to be a comprehensive dictionary of all American toys and games. It is instead *a* dictionary, one of several, not *the* source of all information on these topics. In that, it is similar to other works in the field, many of which are cited in the bibliography.

It strives to be a useful addition to this collection. Efforts were made to list when toys and games debuted in order to set their development in time. Many are no longer being manufactured, but they live on to become another owner's possessions through Internet auctions and face-to-face trading among hobbyists.

The portrayal of items seeks to be good enough to tease the memories of those who fondly, or only vaguely, remember a childhood plaything but do not recall (or perhaps never knew) its proper name. This is especially true for less expensive promotional toys that never came in boxes with accompanying texts. Referred to in the trade as penny or premium prize package toys, they were frequently composed of paper, plastic, or base metal. But their collectible nature belies the material from which they are made.

Included is a supplementary list of individuals important in the American toy industry and a selected bibliography to assist those scholars who wish to pursue additional research on particular topics that they encounter here.

The Dictionary

 Abalone: This is a game of strategy, determination, and skill, like Othello or chess, by the namesake toy company. Abalone is for two players ages eight and up. Black and white marbles (twenty-eight total) face off on either side of a hexagonal playing board. Black always goes first. Players can move one, two, or three marbles sideways or diagonally the distance of one space. The winner is the player who knocks all six of his or her opponent's marbles off the board.

action figures: This is the preferred term for small bendable male figures made for boys' play. Hasbro's G.I. Joe was the first notable "doll" for boys, but Louis Marx & Co. attempted, albeit unsuccessfully, to compete in this area. Marx's military man of the early 1960s, the soldier and paratrooper Stonewall "Stony" Smith, had only somewhat articulated limbs and meager accessories. The All-American Action Fighter Buddy Charlie, in various military gear, was a somewhat better product. Marx then went full force with a frontier theme, introducing the cowboy Johnny West. Jane, Jamie, Jay, Josie, and Janice West followed. Given the relative rarity of female action figures in this era, many of these are quite valuable today. Secret agents also appeared, and in 1975 characters from the comic strip *Archie* (including Veronica, Jughead, and Betty) were made under the Marx name. Tonka's action figures were called Go-Bots. In 1982 Mattel's Masters of the Universe toys appeared at a time when larger-than-life heroes graced the screen in films such as *Conan the Barbarian* (1982), *Conan the Destroyer* (1984), and *The Beastmaster* (1982). Some of these figures delivered punches when one moved their waists. Bandai's Power Rangers, *Star Wars* characters, Mattel's *Simpsons* figures, McFarlane's *Austin Powers* figures, and myriad wrestlers and other sports and combat figures have followed in the path charted by G.I. Joe. *See also* G.I. JOE.

Since the attack on New York's World Trade Center on September 11, 2001, big-calved, Popeye-like, Fisher-Price Rescue Heroes such as the firefighter Billy Blazes have become popular. The company began promoting this series in 1998 unaware that popular opinion would heighten the regard for civil servants in a few years. Blazes' orange-attired work partner Wendy Waters, like Billy, has a backpack, and other accessories such as a bullhorn, ax, fire mask, and helmet. Other figures include Gil Gripper, a scuba diver rescuer, and Sandy Beach, who looks for the drowning and injured aboard his motorized surfboard. Rocky Canyon, a rock climber, helps out hikers and skiers. Cliff Hanger is an air-rescue specialist while Willy Stop is a police officer. Additional characters, whose names give hints to their occupations, include Sam Sparks, Captain Cuffs, Roger Houston, Hal E. Copter, Jake Justice, Aidan Assist, Rip Rockefeller, and Bob Sled. The series imparts a lesson and perhaps career guidance to children who seek stimulation doing positive things. As the label's motto proclaims, these are "cool guys who are good guys." Many of these action figures have videos to show their helping procedures and to teach safety measures.

advertising character dolls: Compiled from *Toy Annual, 2000,* for 1999, p. 17; also from *Toy Shop,* June 30, 2000, p. 10, the following are the top advertising toys if found in mint condition:

1. Quisp bank, Quaker Oats
2. Reddy Kilowatt bobbin' head
3. Mr. Peanut figure, Planters Peanuts
4. Esky store display, *Esquire* magazine, 1940s
5. Elsie the Cow cookie jar, Borden's, 1950s
6. Speedy figure, Alka-Seltzer, 1963
7. Vegetable man display, Kraft, 1980
8. Barnum's Animal Crackers cookie jar, Nabisco, 1972
9. Vegetable man bank, Kraft, 1970s
10. Clark Bar figure, Beatrice Foods, 1960s

Other advertising icons, often with their own dolls, are Buddy Lee (of Lee jeans); Starkist's Charlie Tuna; Bayer Corporation's Speedy (originally known as Sparky) Alka-Seltzer; Bob's Big Boy; the Oscar Meyer Wienermobile; the Motown-singing California Raisins; Gold Seal Company's Mr. Bubble; Planter's Mr. Peanut; Kellogg's Rice

Krispies' Snap, Crackle, and Pop; Kraft's Macaroni and Cheese's C. Rex dinosaur; and the Campbell's Soup Kids. Pillsbury also had Funny Face soft drink mix characters of the 1960s which competed against Kool-Aid's Smiling Pitcher spokesman. Among the Funny Face figures were Rootin' Tootin' Raspberry, Freckle Face Strawberry, Goofy Grape, and "With It" Watermelon. There were also Injun Orange and Chinese Cherry (later more sensitively labeled Jolly-Olly Orange and Choo Choo Cherry).

Aggravation: A Milton Bradley game for ages six and up, this is a classic game of marbles whereby players race their pieces around the board from base to home. Another player can send you back or you can inadvertently send yourself back, causing aggravation.

American Girl: In the 1990s several dolls, most with first and last names, debuted from central periods in American history. Among these were Kaya, a Nez Perce American Indian in 1764; Felicity Merriman from Revolutionary War Virginia of 1774; Josefina Montoya, from what was to become the New Mexico area of 1824; Addy Walker, an African American who escaped from slavery in 1864 with her mother and went North to reunite with the rest of her family; Kirsten Larson, a Swedish immigrant in pioneer Minnesota in 1854; Samantha Parkington, who lived with her wealthy grandmother in 1904; Kit Kittredge, a clever and resourceful Depression Era girl living in Cincinnati in 1934; and Molly McIntyre, a "schemer and a dreamer" whose father is away helping to fight World War II in 1944. These dolls, which emphasized ethnic and economic diversity, important themes in the United States during the 1990s, came with life stories as told in illustrated books. In 2002, the company launched the American Girl Today line with Lindsey Bergman, a Jewish American doll. A three-story building in downtown Chicago, the American Girl Place, is a dedicated site for purchasers of the dolls, books, and accessories. *See* GET REAL GIRL.

Ant Farm: Milton Levine, a Pittsburgh native transplanted to southern California, first marketed Ant Farm in 1956. It is a low-maintenance terrarium consisting of two transparent sheets of plastic in a rectangular green plastic frame accented by a green plastic barn, windmill, and farmhouse and sand that live ants dig through.

Once the buyer purchases this kit, he or she sends in a certificate to Uncle Milton to get all female (which survive in captivity, at least for eight months or so) red harvester ants big enough not to be able to escape through air holes at the top of the container. Harvester ants are also one of the few species that digs during daylight hours. Schools and museums applauded this gentle initiation to the science of entomology, and science museums are important vendors of them. In 1969 Uncle Milton issued an Ant Farm board game.

Antiques Roadshow–The Game: Antiques Roadshow—The Game is based on the popular WGBH–Boston produced and Chubb Insurance underwritten PBS television series that debuted in the United States in 1996. The American program is modeled after the British series on air since 1976. This game, intended for two to four adult players, has been a Hasbro offering since 2000. As on the program, people appraise whether items are genuine and valuable antiques or less expensive reproductions. The kit contains 162 Antique Cards with actual histories of the items; forty Value Cards; thirty-two Antique Speak cards, containing jargon that appraisers use; a display board and cardboard tokens; a plastic easel; and instructions, all in a metal tin for easy portability.

Contestants choose which out of two stated origins of an item on an Antique Card is correct—actual antique or imitation. Play commences with four participants with each receiving four Antique Cards; with three players, each gets six cards; and with two players, each gets eight cards. All Antique Cards are set picture side up (and history side down). In all scenarios, players receive three Antique Speak Cards (set face down) and ten Value Cards. Honesty is expected on the show as well as in play. Contestants who already know the history and value of an item on their Antique Cards should call attention to that fact and replace them with other cards from the deck. In turn, each player selects an Antique Card without anyone seeing the story on the back and displays it on the easel. All players select a Value Card that he or she thinks will most closely approximate that of the exhibited item. Players with Antique Speak cards containing words matching those on the exhibited card discard them. Players who choose the actual appraised value of the displayed item also jettison their respective Value Card.

The game continues until one or more participants dispose of all their cards. As in reality, there can be more than one winner (or correct appraiser). This game appeals to PBS viewers, bargain hunters, and savvy investors.

Ants in the Pants: Invented by Herb Schaper, who also came up with the game Cootie, this Milton Bradley game is for ages three to six years and for two to four players. The object is to get all the play ants in your color to jump into the plastic pants container to win. The set includes a pants game container, suspenders, and sixteen ants.

Aristoplay: This is an educational card game by a company whose first product was Greek Myths and Legends for two or more players ages seven and up. It was designed to help junior high school students learn while playing rummy using cards with thirteen Greek myths and legends. Other games were variations of the nineteenth-century game Authors with separate card decks for American and children's authors. Aristoplay is also the manufacturer of Quick Pix flash card games. *See* QUICK PIX.

baby dolls: First introduced commercially in the early nineteenth century, they largely replaced dolls more severely dressed as adults. The London Crystal Palace Exhibition of 1851 displayed baby dolls, often with more natural rubber faces than was previously the case.

Baby Tender Love: Mattel's 1970s line of dolls included one that gave the imitation of a sneeze, Baby Brother Tender Love, and a version that made a kissing expression when its stomach was squeezed.

backgammon: A centuries-old board game of strategy, probability, intuition, and psychology, like chess, backgammon is a game of visual patterns engaged in one on one between two opposing sides. It is played with dice (one pair of dice for each side) and counters (fifteen on each side) in which each contestant attempts to be the first to gather his or her pieces into one corner by moving around a track divided into twenty-four daggerlike divisions (points). A center partition known as a bar cuts the board in two. Once in the corner, a player removes his or her pieces (bears them off) from the board.

Some of the nomenclature used include gammon-double game-won if a player bears off all fifteen of his or her men before the opponent bears off a single man; backgammon-triple game—won if a player bears off all fifteen of his or her pieces before the opponent bears off one and he or she still has one or more on his or her home board or bar; doubling cube—a six-sided die marked with the numerals 2, 4, 8, 16, 32, and 64 used to keep track of the number of units at stake in each game. A single piece, or counter, on a point is called a blot; two or more pieces on a point form a block.

The click and rattle of the dice and the sound of the round game pieces as they move about the board are part of the evocative appeal of this game (similar to the slap of mah-jongg tiles). Most backgammon sets come in attaché cases (some quite high scale in felt and leather) which can be folded up for use in parks, at clubs, or while traveling. The basic goals can be learned rather quickly, but many players develop complex strategies over years of practice.

balloons: For centuries, people in both the Old and New Worlds filled animal bladders and intestines with either water or air for use as playthings. In 1783 the French Montgolfier brothers demonstrated their discovery of a hot-air balloon. This set off an aeronautics craze among well-to-do and scientifically inclined adults. The English scientist Michael Faraday in 1824 was credited with making the first rubber balloon. This nonvulcanized version was coated on the inside with flour to prevent the sides from sticking together. In 1825 rubber manufacturer Thomas Hancock introduced a kit with which one could construct a toy balloon similar to Faraday's. Toy balloons, unaffected by temperature changes using Charles Goodyear's method of vulcanization, were first made in 1847 by J. G. Ingram of London.

This popular party and carnival favor for children, in its rubber or latex form, usually spherical in shape, was inflated by either air or helium (which caused it to rise). Adults also used it for advertising purposes, as they utilized the even larger surfaces afforded by blimps. There are some caveats regarding rubber balloons. Parents or guardians should closely supervise their charges because balloons, which could be swallowed when not inflated, are the most dangerous toys for children up to age eight. They are environmentally unsound as well, for they generally are not biodegradable (and for this reason are no longer deliberately released en masse at festivals). Long balloons can be creatively twisted into animal shapes. Despite their hidden dangers, however, the unassailable attraction of children for them is emphasized by the perennially popular French film *The Red Balloon* (1956). In this classic movie, the director Albert Lamorisse was able to convey the friendship between an often-bullied young boy in Paris and a giant balloon.

In recent years, foil balloons, especially those printed with character faces or birthday or holiday greetings, appeared. These inflatable objects are a by-product of NASA's space missions. They are composed of nylon sheets coated on one side with polyethylene and a metallic compound on the other.

balsa planes: Invented by World War I U.S. Navy Ensign Paul Guillow in light of the popularity of Charles Lindbergh's solo, non-stop transatlantic flight in 1927, these lightweight planes first had to be cut out of patterns using an X-acto blade. In the early 1940s Guillow introduced easier versions that only needed slipping a wing through the plane's body and carefully twisting a rubber band to give it flight. During World War II, balsa wood was needed for lift rafts and a foam version was substituted.

banks: As collectibles, banks fall into the categories of mechanical, still, and registering. Mechanical banks are triggered into brief movement by the fall of a coin through a slot. Made at first of cast iron in 1869 and in the early twentieth century of lithographed tin, and since World War II often of plastic, since 1958 banks have had a society devoted to them—the Mechanical Bank Collectors of America. Still banks, as their name implies, do not move. Plastic figural banks, often of cartoon characters, have been popular in the post–World War II period. Registering banks are often shaped like a cash register, adding machine, or a small bank building. They usually have dials that display the amount (of coins) put into them and are reset when the coin box is opened.

Among some significant late nineteenth-century mechanical banks are Jonah and the Whale, Shepard Hardware's Humpty Dumpty, and the Hubley Ferris Wheel. The J. & E. Stevens Co. of Cromwell, Connecticut, manufactured a great many products including the Fowler (Hunter) bank and the "Dark Town Battery Bank." This last offering, first issued in 1888, was notable in its straightforward, nonderogatory, depiction of three African Americans playing baseball at a time when the sport was not generally segregated. Other popular mechanical banks include Uncle Sam dropping coins into a carpetbag; Theodore Roosevelt shooting a coin into a bear's mouth; a dog performing the trick of jumping through a hoop to place a coin in a small barrel. Many mechanical banks that purport to be of a late nineteenth-century vintage are in fact expert reproductions. This presents a challenge to collectors of authentic items but a boon to those who merely want these objects as keepsakes or working models.

Barbie: Mattel's perennially popular high-fashion doll, the adaptation by Ruth and Elliott Handler (who, together with a business partner, Harold Mattson, had previously founded Mattel Toys in Hawthorne, California) of a European doll. The Handlers named the doll after their daughter in 1959 (and her companion Ken after their son in 1961). Barbie's predecessor appeared in Switzerland and Germany in the 1950s as Lilli, a provocative sweater-clad figure marketed to men as automobile dash decor. In 1952 Reinhard Beuthien created a full-figured female for the newspaper *Bild-Zeitung*. After drawing many cartoons of Lilli, Beuthien designed a doll in 1955 with the assistance of Max Weissbrodt. This doll had the basic characteristics of Barbie: almond-shaped eyes, a high forehead, high breasts, and a thin neck.

The Handlers were inspired after a skiing vacation to introduce Barbie to the United States as a girls' fashion plaything. This allowed young girls to fantasize in three dimensions, for Barbie initially walked in the steps of dress-up paper dolls. Ruth Handler in fact claimed that Barbie offered a less cumbersome version of paper dolls. Still, the new doll met initial resistance from mothers who were reluctant to buy a figure with breasts and with more than anatomically correct measurements.

Over the years Barbie has proven to be controversial not only for her unrealistic physical proportions but for her penchant for the glamorous life and her rebellion against domesticity. According to some critics, she encouraged consumerism (and accordingly wasteful ways). Purportedly, Barbie did not teach girls the traditional nurturing skills that most dolls historically did; she influenced them to associate independence with acquisitiveness. Adding on the outfits, accessories (such as houses and cars), and doll companions meant spending much more money than the initial purchase of the doll itself. In this way, Barbie merged with the fashion trends of the late 1950s and 1960s, which saw an emphasis on accessorizing.

Barbie was an exaggerated teenager with no visible parental ties, although true aficionados, with some digging, have discovered that her parents are named George and Margaret and that she went to Willow High School where she met her companion/accessory Ken Carson. Barbie later got a younger sister, Skipper, in 1964 (the same year that Allan, a friend of Ken's, appeared). By the same token, she has been highly profitable because of her numerous cars and other accoutrements. Little known to most collectors, she does have a last name—Roberts—and a middle name—Millicent. But her fame means that Barbie is known worldwide just by her first name.

Barbie's quick success also prompted Mattel to enter the game business, albeit only as a sideline. In the 1960s the company produced the games Barbie's Keys to Fame (1963) and Barbie, Queen of the Prom (1960). The winner of the latter game became president of a school club, bought an evening dress with her baby-sitting money, and found a steady boyfriend. In 1964 Barbie's little sister Skipper got her own game based on a girl's dream of owning a horse. *See* MY LITTLE PONY.

Barbie acquired friends such as the freckle-faced Midge in 1963, Francie (actually introduced as a cousin) in 1966, Stacey in 1968, and a black friend named Christie in the same year. In 1995 Baby Sister Kelly appeared (evidence, perhaps, that her seldom-seen parents are still flourishing). The year 1997 witnessed the manifestation of Share a Smile Becky, a disabled friend in a wheelchair. Barbie's impact on the doll industry has been tremendous. She rapidly reduced the share of baby dolls and inspired imitators such as Ideal's Tammy (who had Mom and Dad dolls and also games based on her), American Character's Tressy (with hair that grew when it was pulled out of her head), and Topper's Penny Brite.

In 1960, Barbie's fashion model pout softened a bit. In 1967, Barbie received mod clothes, a longer face, eyelashes that were longer, and a twist-and-turn waist. From 1968 until 1972 Barbie and many of her companions appeared in versions with pull strings that allowed them to talk. This attested to the wide popularity of the Chatty Cathy line of dolls. It was also a way to have the dolls interact, albeit marginally, with their owners. Barbie, Christie, and others' conversation was rather basic and superficial, mostly about parties and the opposite sex. That and the fact that most of these mechanisms soon stopped working led to their discontinuation.

In 1971, the tanned and smiling Malibu Barbie appeared. In 1977, Barbie's smile widened, showing many teeth, and she came already wearing a dress instead of a one-piece swimsuit (which originally was zebra-striped).

In the 1980s and 1990s, Barbie assumed a more serious disposition, becoming interested in formerly male professions such as dentistry and athletics. But in 1992, Mattel upset women's groups when its Teen Talk Barbie claimed that "math class is tough." The controversy made the doll a winner among collectors. In 1997 Movin' Groovin' Barbie, a striped-garbed doll that could be made to walk when held with a special handle, appeared. In 1998, Mattel introduced a Barbie alternative with more realistic proportions and in August 2000 a version with a belly button and a bendable waist. This is not the same Barbie featured running for president that year. Also in 2000 was the Barbie Bake with Me Oven with a working oven very similar to the classic Easy-Bake Oven. A Barbie Hall of Fame is owned by Evelyn Burkhalter in Palo Alto, California. *See also* KEN.

Barrel of Monkeys: In 1966 Lakeside Industries of Minneapolis, Minnesota, introduced this gender-neutral multicolored collection of twelve plastic monkeys in a plastic barrel. The monkeys can be an assortment of yellow, blue, red, and green or sometimes all one color. It is appropriate for ages three and up. The barrel is either red, yellow, or blue. The challenge is to see how many of the play animals with extended arms and legs you can hook together in one string when pulling them out of a pile laid out on a flat surface. This toy, which exercises fine hand-eye control, became a perennial pastime for baby boomers in their childhoods and continues to be popular with many as a stress reliever in their adult years. It is currently marketed by Hasbro.

Basic Fun: This company is a manufacturer of miniature working toy key chains. Many of these are officially licensed versions of classic games, such as Barrel of Monkeys, Battleship, Cootie, Don't Break the Ice, Mousetrap, Operation, Ouija, Perfection, Scrabble, and Twister that one can actually play. Others such as Boggle, Clue,

Monopoly, Trouble, and Yahtzee come with just a few pieces. There are mini versions of the Duncan Yo-Yo, Etch A Sketch, Frisbee, Magic 8 Ball, Mrs. Potato Head, Radio Flyer Wagon, 1960s-style Schwinn Krate banana-seated bicycles, Slinky Pets, Superball (high bouncing), View-Master, and Wooly Willy. There are also character key chains, among them Austin Powers, Barbie, CatDog, Pokemon, and the Powerpuff Girls.

battery-operated toys: Shortly after World War II the Japanese introduced the world market to battery-operated toys intended to move rather than merely light up. American companies, especially in the period up to the late 1960s, entered heavily into the competition, with space-age toys proving to be particularly popular. Since that time, batteries for toys has been such a fact of life that well-equipped Christmas gift givers need to be stocked with this commodity. One problem for vintage toy collectors has been corrosion in battery cases when batteries are left in toys stored in attics and basements.

Battle of the Sexes: Introduced in 2001 by University Games, for ages twelve and up, this quiz game, in board and card game formats, is played with gender-based questions, that is, responses stereotypically more likely to be known by someone in a male or a female position. Designed for two or more participants, sides are arranged by gender. Male cards are blue and female are pink and questions are read by their gender opposites. Each card contains three questions and during a turn a side can respond correctly to up to three answers before the other team proceeds. The first team to win two cards by answering a total of six questions correctly wins.

Some examples of the male-oriented questions, How many lugs are there on a wheel? Who is the famous alter ego of Australian actor Paul Hogan? In which game can you hit a "mulligan"? Queries posed by women to men: How does one stop a run in a stocking? Name two of the four March sisters in *Little Women*. What color is chartreuse a shade of?

Battleship, the Classic Naval Combat Game: Battleship was originally a paper and pencil game published in 1931 as Salvo by the Starex Novelty Co. In 1933 the Strathmore Co. published it as Combat, the Battleship Game. Battleship first appeared in its present form in 1967 as a Milton Bradley item. Milton Bradley last copyrighted it in 1990 and it is still available from that division of Hasbro. In this contest based on strategy and luck, each of two players aged seven or above gets five plastic ships. They consist of aircraft carriers, battleships, cruisers, submarines, and destroyers. The players sit facing each other so neither can see the other's ocean grid on the raised lids of their game units. They place their ships either horizontally or vertically on their grids, identified by letter and number coordinates. They hope that they will not get hit, but they still try to sink their opponent's pieces. Players fire shots by calling out a number and letter. The opponent must indicate whether the shot is a hit or a miss, that is, whether the other player correctly guessed coordinates of a ship. If a ship is hit, a red peg is placed on the grid at those coordinates, the peg set into the tops of the plastic representations of these ships. White pegs are placed in corresponding coordinates that are misses (that is, incorrectly called out as locations of vessels) so that a player does not announce that location again. The loser is the one who suffers the deprivation of all of his or her pieces. In 1989 a small travel version appeared, and in 2002 the electronic version was released.

BB guns: Although technically not a toy, metal pellet guns have been used by boys as a preparation for and an introduction to regular firearms, just as toys have served to introduce children to other adult activities. In 1885, the Markham Air Rifle Co. became one of the first to market this product in the United States. In 1888, the Plymouth Iron Windmill Co. made a Daisy air rifle based on a design submitted by Clarence Hamilton. Based on the success of this product, the firm renamed itself, becoming the Daisy Manufacturing Co. in 1895. Daisy bought out Markham as well as others of its competitors.

The "BB" stands for ball bearing, which is what the metal pellets resembled. Daisy Manufacturing produced similar products beginning in the 1930s, such as the Buck Rogers ray guns and Red Ryder guns, both based on comic strip heroes. The much-acclaimed film *A Christmas Story* (1983) told a heartwarming tale of the boy Ralphie growing up in the 1940s who finally received the object of his desire—a Red Ryder air gun. This was accompanied by his parents' misgivings about the gift.

Daisy Manufacturing moved to Rogers, Arkansas, in 1957 and remains the world's oldest and largest manufacturer of these less-than-lethal but still potentially hazardous weapons. The early 1970s witnessed the introduction of Airsoft pistols, which use light rubber BBs instead of metal pellets. Since 1988, the barrels of the guns have been fitted with orange tips, presumably to lend a greater measure of safety.

(Classic) Bead Maze: A visually stimulating and therapeutic (even for adults) pastime intended by Educo International for children eighteen months to five years of age, this is a favorite in doctors' waiting rooms where it engages sometimes impatient children, to the relief of their parents. The Bead Maze develops hand-eye and coordination skills. It consists of brightly colored wooden beads that children guide over plastic-covered wires mounted on a wooden base.

Beanie Babies: These are small, plush, understuffed, and hence floppy and huggable toy animals first merchandised in 1993 by Ty, Inc. of Oak Brook, Illinois. The creation of H. Ty Warner, a former Midwest salesman for Dakin, a defunct San Francisco toy manufacturer, Beanie Babies are sold in gift shops and toy stores. The line includes almost 200 characters. In 1996, some Beanie Babies were "retired" (ceased being made for the first time). This made them more valuable as collectors' items. The accumulation of the earlier Care Bears and later Beanie Babies conveys a sense of abundance and a comforting, cuddly feeling of security. In addition, accumulating and ordering collectibles can convey a sense of mastery and train the mind, especially when selectivity and judgment come into play.

Some Beanie Babies, such as the Princess Diana memorial teddy bear, have been used to raise money for charity. Although their popularity waned somewhat, Beanies made a resurgence with Righty the Elephant and Lefty the Donkey in the 2000 election year. As a portent of the outcome in the electoral college, Righty sold the best.

Beatles "Flip Your Wig": In 1964, Milton Bradley rushed to cash in on the Fab Four's sudden popularity in the United States with what turned out to be a little-known game with them as a theme. A resurgence in Beatlemania began at the end of the twentieth century, making this piece quite a collectible.

Bendies: This is the current generic term for rubbery play figures without articulated joints. The Claymation figures of Gumby and

Pokey in the 1950s were the precursors of a great many characters, mostly based on television and film personalities. In the 1960s, Lakeside Industries of Minneapolis, Minnesota, produced them in versions for the home market. The Kohner Brothers produced Shapees (related to the same manufacturer's Loony Links) which are soft plastic round and square pieces that fit together like beads to form animate objects. Current Bendies figures include those based on the Nickelodeon television network's CatDog and films such as *Planet of the Apes, The Rocky Horror Picture Show, Star Trek, Aladdin, The Nightmare Before Christmas* characters (including Jack Skellington, Sally, Pajama Jack, and the mayor). Lines such as Bend-ems and Bendos of the 1990s are priced below comparable action figure toys, making them more appealing to kids who actually buy their own playthings.

In 1965 Mattel introduced Liddle Kiddles, a bendable toy line that expanded rapidly with resonant names such as Peter Pandiddle, Freezy Sliddle, Calamity Jiddle, Liddle Miss Muffet, and Little Red Riding Kiddle. In 1967 there were Skididdle Kiddles, with attached walkers, Jewelry Kiddles, and Kiddle Kolognes (dolls in perfume bottle containers). In 1968, Mattel followed these with Kiddle Kones and Lollipops (dolls enclosed in facsimile ice cream cones or lollipops); Circus Animiddle Kiddles; Story Book Kiddles; and *Chitty Chitty Bang Bang* Kiddles based on characters in the film. *See* GUMBY AND POKEY.

Benny Goodman Swings into a Game of Musical Information: In the 1940s Toy Creations introduced this musical quiz game featuring a xylophone and questions about popular songs.

Betsy McCall: A pre-Barbie fashion doll, she originally appeared as a paper doll in the monthly *McCall's* magazine for women. American Character of New York later produced Betsy as a vinyl doll in 8-, 14-, 20-, 30-, and 36-inch heights. She carried a wrist tag that said that she was from the pages of *McCall's*. Other companies produced variants of Betsy including the Robert Tonner Doll Company in 1996.

Betsy Wetsy: This doll from Ideal, introduced in 1954, cried and wet from water fed by a bottle. Betsy Wetsy had accessories such as a wind-up swing and a bathtub. American Character's Tiny Tears is a variant of this doll.

bicycles: Two-wheeled conveyances used for recreation and transportation, bicycles in one form or another have been around since the late eighteenth century. One version in the mid-nineteenth century had no pedals and looked like a hobby horse. With wooden wheels and uncomfortable seats, the nickname "boneshaker" was apt. In the late 1870s, a version of the bicycle with a large front wheel (to traverse the maximum length possible without the more efficient indirect drive provided by the 1890s' innovation of a bicycle chain) and a smaller rear wheel proved to be so popular that it was called the "ordinary." Alternate names for it were the high-wheeler or, in Great Britain, the penny farthing.

In addition to a bicycle chain, which allowed for two wheels of equal size, the 1890s saw the widespread use of pneumatic tires, introduced the previous decade. Popular American brands included Pope of Hartford, Connecticut, and Boston, Massachusetts, and Columbia and Schwinn of Chicago. Tricycles, popular both for women in billowing skirts and for children, had three wheels. The 1960s saw a curious amalgam for children of earlier forms with the Big Wheel. This was a low, sit-down three-wheel, chainless, plastic tricycle with the pedals directly connected to the front wheel (a kind of low-wheeler tricycle). The 1970s witnessed modern "alternative" versions, introduced more for their iconoclastic attractions than for their practicality. There were banana-shaped and elevated seats and elongated handlebars, as well as slick or treadless tires. Recumbent bicycles, especially comfortable for the baby-boomer generation, actually had made their appearance among the profusion of bicycle innovations at the turn of the previous century.

bisque dolls: Made of unglazed porcelain appearing in shades of white to rosy pink, these dolls, in the nineteenth century largely made in Germany, often had holes in their crowns to reduce their weight and also to lessen import duties. These dolls usually had blue eyes and most frequently black hair to lend ample contrast with the whiteness of their faces. By the 1860s, bisque dolls, which are fired twice with color added after the first firing, had largely replaced the less lifelike China dolls. Bisque dolls were made for careful child play but now are primarily issued as character collectibles.

bobble heads (also known as bobbin' head dolls, nodding heads, wobbly heads, nodders, and wobblers): Often used by adults for car dashboard or rear-window ornaments, these figures were popular in plastic or bisque during the 1950s and 1960s. They experienced a revival in the late 1990s when they mostly depicted celebrities in the fields of professional baseball, football, basketball, and hockey, as well as television stars, advertising icons, political figures, and cartoon characters. Bobbles actually first were made in limited quantities in the United States in bisque during the nineteenth century. Temple nodders, often seated figures of Buddha, appeared in Asia in the seventeenth century. Variations of the American versions consist of animals with tails as well as heads that move. Among the most popular wobblers at the dawn of the twenty-first century were Reddy Kilowatt, Betty Boop, Rat Fink, Space Ace, and Felix the Cat but more figures, especially retro ones, appear all the time.

A rival to the bobble head craze, putting the faces of sports and other figures on rubber ducks became noticeable in mid-2002 (although the company Celebriducks first promoted the concept several years earlier). According to company president Craig Wolf, he is building on the friendly feeling that many Americans have for the rubber ducks from their childhoods, rather than marketing his product in a cultural vacuum.

Boggle: A game of logic and visual recognition from Parker Brothers for ages eight and up first released in 1973, Boggle is played with a small container holding sixteen cubes (four letters by four letters), each marked with a different letter on each of its six sides. A player shakes the container, watches the cubes land, and finds as many words of three or more letters as possible within three minutes (a timer is included). Points accumulate based on word length. Players can find words within words and can continue as long as they like (not taking longer than three minutes each turn). Words do not count if they are used by more than one player. Participants earn from three to eleven points, one point for each letter of a word. Boggle Jr., also from Parker Brothers, is for ages three to six. Players attempt to spell words that match displayed pictures. Children learn the lessons of object and word recognition, sorting and grouping, concentration and memory, and taking turns. Big Boggle has a grid with five letters by five letters. Body Boggle (1984) is like Twister, and physically interactive. Players spell words on a floor mat. A CD-ROM version of Boggle appeared in 1997.

Book of Knowledge Electromatic Dial Quiz: In 1961 Transogram produced a game with a large plastic dial and dual scorekeepers which lit up when a player selected the correct answer. In 1964 it was renamed You Are Right!

blocks: Didactic playthings that scholars have recommended for children at least since the seventeenth century, these usually wooden squares were first mass produced in the nineteenth century. Philosopher John Locke, the founder of the kindergarten Friedrich Froebel, and twentieth-century child specialists Luther Gulick and Benjamin Spock all praised the creativity and intellectual development that simple building blocks elicited in children. In 1867, Charles Crandall of New York, a wooden goods manufacturer, introduced his interlocking "tongue and groove" line, a predecessor to Lego's blocks. In 1874, Crandall debuted Expression Blocks which children used to form facial expressions by combining the blocks. In 1877 Crandall promoted his Wide Awake Blocks. Bissell Blocks are lithographed wooden blocks with building designs. *See* LEGO TOYS *for information on a variety of less free-form blocks.*

"brain games": Educational games have been prominent since the mid-nineteenth century. Perhaps due to the popularity of television quiz shows, quite a few appeared in the 1950s and 1960s. In 1955 *Today Show* host Dave Garraway introduced a game where players bought and sold entire states (which was much more of a real estate deal than Monopoly could provide) called Dave Garraway's Game of Possession, made by Athletic Products. One of many place-name quiz games was GEO-graphy by Cadaco-Ellis in 1954. Parker Brothers had similar series, including 1947's Game of States and Cities, 1952's Game of State Capitals, and 1956's Game of the States. Milton Bradley had its own in 1960 with its Game of the States. Players learned state capitals and natural resources. In that same year Milton Bradley introduced Go to the Head of the Class as well as Know the Stars and Planets. In 1962 Selchow & Righter produced Game of Heroes and Events and Game of Products and Resources.

In 1959 Jacmar's Mr. Brain invited children to feed answers into a computer's mouth. Its eyes indicated whether they got the answer right. In 1960 Hasbro produced an early affordable light blue plastic computer for kids called the Think-A-Tron. This "machine that thinks like a man" had flashing lights and punch cards with questions so that players could test the machine's knowledge. Following in the manner of real-world computers, in 1968 Hasbro updated its Think-A-Tron as the Mark 106 Computer. Also in 1960 Hasbro also produced Mentor, the "'Man of Bronze' who thinks for himself" whom the player sought to challenge. Other educational games are listed under their own names.

Bratz dolls: MGA Entertainment's hot seller of the Christmas 2002 season is a series of sensuous-lipped dolls with hip and funky attitudes, a made-up look, and belly-baring clothing to match. They are all 10 inches tall (about 2 inches given to the heads, so they are larger than Barbie's and made to be easier for young hands to play with). The mini versions of each character are 4.5 inches tall. Rather than changing shoes, which can get lost, the owner snaps off the feet that are combined with the boots or chunky shoes, rather than high heels. The legs are bendable. Among these dolls are females Cloe, Jade, Sasha, Yasmin, and Meygan as well as males Cameron, Koby, Eitan, and Dylan, with undoubtedly more to follow. Curiously, like the contemporary Rescue Heroes, Bratz dolls sport wide lower legs, as if perpetually wearing bell bottoms. *See* DIVA STARZ.

bubble pipes: Franz Hals and other seventeenth-century Flemish painters attest to the fact that children in their time blew bubbles from clay pipes. In the twentieth century, marketers of bubble products commercialized them. Character bubble toys, especially Disney characters and later Mr. Potato Head and *Sesame Street* images, were popular. Mickey Mouse and his cohorts were popular beginning in the 1930s when bar soap was still the normal bubble source. In the 1940s, Chemtoy sold a liquid soap bubble solution. Tootsietoy (a division of Strombecker Corporation since 1926) acquired that franchise in 1979. Mr. Bubbles is its trademark for bubble wands as well as pipes although Morris Plastics Corp. marketed a Mr. Bubbles plastic turtle which blew bubbles when a child squeezed its belly.

Always a peaceful activity, and certainly an evocation of cleanliness, during the antiestablishment 1960s adults also found relaxation in blowing bubbles. Imperial (started by Fred Kort from Strombecker in 1969), Wells, and Pustifix were purveyors of bubble solution in the last third of the twentieth century. David Stein's Bubble Thing produced a massive fifty-foot-long bubble.

Burp Gun: In 1955 Mattel introduced this gun that uses caps and produces a loud noise and smoke on *The Mickey Mouse Club* television program. This made it the first toy advertised on nationwide television (just as Mr. Potato Head was earlier the first to receive that honor on a local network). Another version by the same name uses air to safely expel up to fifteen Ping-Pong type balls either one at a time or in a collective burst.

Cabbage Patch Kids dolls: Soft body dolls with homely plastic faces, presumably with one-of-a-kind facial expressions that were marketed to be "adopted" with papers rather than purchased, Cabbage Patch Kids were the creation of Xavier Roberts of rural Cleveland, Georgia. Coleco industries mass marketed them in the Christmas season of 1983 when they created near riots at toy stores. Coleco, previously burned by the abrupt drop in the video game industry, expanded rapidly to meet the demand for the doll and then went under. Soon thereafter Pound Puppies, a canine version of the Cabbage Patch concept, appeared under the auspices of other manufacturers. This was an adoptable toy dog from a pound that was a socially acceptable "doll" for nurturing little boys. Hasbro later purchased Coleco and it continues the lines of Cabbage Patch Kids. *See* POUND PUPPIES.

Candy Land: The classic children's game was devised by Eleanor Abbott, a woman recovering in bed from polio who wanted to develop a way to occupy children who had the same disease. It was first offered in 1949 by Milton Bradley and is geared toward helping children age three and up learn numbers and colors. There is no reading involved. Two, three, or four players draw one of sixty-four cards to move gingerbread men–like character pieces around a board. Players get to move through idyllic spots such as Peppermint Stick Forest,

Lollipop Woods, and Gumdrop Mountain and past the Crooked Old Peanut Brittle House and Molasses Swamp. The winner is the first to pass through all of these areas, often facilitated by lucky landings on spots with shortcuts (that is, the Rainbow Trail and Gumdrop Pass). The end of the game is achieved when the first player reaches Candy Castle. There is now a Winnie-the-Pooh version of this game.

cap guns: Cap guns were made in the late 1860s by gun manufacturers who had factories idled by the end of the American Civil War and who wanted to use up their inventories of gunpowder. Manufacturers created paper rolls with small dots filled with gunpowder that could be loaded into toy guns and rifles. When fired, the paper caps made a loud noise and emitted a bit of smoke. Children often did without the toy guns, blasting the caps by directly pounding them with rocks. The smell emitted is evocative of childhood much as the scent of Play-Doh and Crayola crayons conveys childhood to many boys and girls.

Captain Video: In 1950 Milton Bradley produced a game based on this pioneering television program that debuted in 1949 on the DuMont Network. The game had a spaceship's instrument panel as its design. This proved a prototype for other games geared to the outer-space craze of the 1950s and 1960s. Among them were Space Pilot in 1951 by Cadaco-Ellis; Steve Scott Space Scout by Transogram in 1951 (named in honor of company president Charles Raizen's newborn grandson); *Leave It to Beaver* Rocket to the Moon in 1959 by Hasbro; Orbit by Parker Brothers in 1959; *Buck Rogers* by Transogram in 1965; *Lost in Space* by Milton Bradley in 1965; and *Star Trek,* based on the initially relatively unpopular television program, in 1966.

cartoon tie-ins: *See* ADVERTISING CHARACTER DOLLS.

Cashflow: Author Robert Kiyosaki, who was born and raised in Hawaii, told through his books (such as *Rich Dad, Poor Dad: What the Rich Teach Their Kids About Money—That the Poor and Middle Class Do Not,* 1998) that it is better and safer to be an investor than to work for someone else. He invented the board game Cashflow to teach secrets that only the rich know about money, accounting, and investing. Cashflow comes in several versions, including Cashflow 101 (for beginners), Cashflow 202 (for those who have mastered

101), Cashflow for Kids, and a Windows-based computer game called Cashflow the E-Game.

***The Cat in the Hat* Game:** Introduced by University Games in 1997, this game is for two to four players ages four and up. It comes with a game board, forty picture cards, four playing pieces and stands, a spinner card, and an instruction manual. As players move around collecting picture cards, they learn letter and color recognition by matching the color of cards to the color of spaces on the board. The object is to amass the most picture cards, an action comparable to gathering up items scattered all over the house. The game concludes when the last player reaches the finish line. The player at that time with the most picture cards wins. In 2003 University Games premiered a movie edition which was essentially the same but was tied in to the film released that year.

celluloid dolls: Celluloid was the name for a highly flammable form of plastic trademarked in the United States in 1870 by John Wesley Hyatt, a prolific inventor. Celluloid, the first successful synthetic plastic, was originally composed of the materials cellulose nitrate and powdered camphor. In 1891 Hyatt absorbed other competitors and reorganized as The Celluloid Manufacturing Company. German, American, French, and Japanese doll makers all used this material despite its combustible nature and tendency to fade with time. Although frequently marketed as unbreakable, celluloid was actually only relatively so. Unlike bisque and china dolls, those made of celluloid did not shatter. Unlike composition dolls, they did not peel.

In 1907, fireproof celluloid first appeared. Celluloid was used as a substitute for ivory in billiard balls, combs, and knife handles, as well as for figural toys such as dolls. Other plastics had largely replaced it by the 1950s.

character dolls: These are dolls based primarily on recognizable real people or on fictional figures. Emblematic of the first group is the Shirley Temple doll of the 1930s with its corkscrew curls, dimpled smile, and polka-dot dress. The Lone Ranger and Hopalong Cassidy figures of the 1950s epitomize the latter group. More modern versions of character dolls, presumably intended for an adult audience, are caricatured images of politicians.

Charades for Dummies: Introduced by Pressman in 1998, this game requires three to four players ages twelve and up. There are four types of cards: Charade Cards containing one to four words that holders have to act out; Tip Cards, which are all good, and allow players to advance a certain number of spaces; Judgment Cards, which are a mixture of good and bad; and Warning Cards, which are all bad, and require movement backward. The board contains five different kinds of spaces: Start/Finish, Safe, Tip, Judgment, and Warning Spots requiring the players landing on them to take one of those respective cards. Play begins when a participant draws a Charade Card. All other players shout out responses. The correct guesser advances one space and the charades actor goes back a space if no one guesses his or her word. The first person to cross the finish line wins.

Chatty Cathy: Introduced by Mattel in 1960 as its first talking doll, this 20-inch, freckle-faced, blue-eyed, vinyl doll with blonde bangs had a repertoire of eleven phrases, any one of which she would say when one pulled her Chatty Ring in the back. In 1961, Mattel introduced the first variant, Talking Matty Mattel, and Chatty Baby and Charmin' Chatty, "the educated doll," soon followed in 1962. She stereotypically wore dark-rimmed glasses and a serious sailing outfit. Charmin' Chatty could speak 120 different phrases issuing from interchangeable records that were inserted in her left side. Also in the Mattel line of talking dolls, but tied in with the television program *Family Affair,* was Talking Mrs. Beasley with its distinctive square-lensed eyeglasses.

checkers: A game played on a board with sixty-four (in the United States) traditionally red and black alternating squares. Boards are often foldable and reversible. Each of two players begins with twelve round disks, usually all red or black but sometimes black and white. Pieces can move forward diagonally until they reach the opposite side. By doing this, they are "crowned" with another piece on top and can move both backward and forward. By jumping his or her opponent's piece, the opposing player removes it. The loser is the player without any pieces. Draws occur when neither player can force a win.

Checkered boards have been found in ancient Egyptian tombs and on Greek pottery, and were used for backgammon, chess, and other ancient games as well. Checkers can also be played with thirty-two,

100 (especially in Europe), and 144 (especially in Canada) squares. The American Checkers Federation now calls a green and yellow checkerboard the official version, perhaps to differentiate serious tournaments from other games.

chess: A challenge (indeed, more than a game) for two people confronted on a checkerboard. Each player moves his or her sixteen pieces according to particular protocols. The winner is the person who successfully threatens (checkmates) the other's king, no matter how many pieces he or she has left. The king is the only piece that cannot be removed from the board until the game ends. The named pieces (king, queen, rook [castle], bishop, knight, pawn) reflects the game development in medieval Europe although it probably originated in the East. Each player has one king and queen; two rooks, bishops, and knights; and eight pawns, all with their own types of permitted movements. In effect, the two sides represent opposing armies.

Chinese checkers: A board game played with marbles on a six-pointed star with holes to contain the pieces, Chinese checkers originated in Europe in the late nineteenth century but acquired its current moniker from J. Pressman in 1928. The popularity of mah-jongg may have indicated that an "exotic" name would help in marketing. A craze during the 1930s, Milton Bradley and L.G. Ballard also produced versions of Chinese checkers. Anywhere from two to six players can play with a set of usually ten colored marbles (or plastic pegs) at the star's points. A player can move one spot (step) or jump over (hop) his or her own or any number of his or her opponents' pieces (as in checkers), but he or she does not capture the hopped-over pieces (unlike in checkers). The winner is the first player to get all of his or her pieces to the other side of the board.

Chop Stix: The Oriental Stacking Game: A game like Jenga, Chop Stix is for players ages seven and up. One or more can play. There are seventy wooden logs, three pairs of chopsticks (and one pair of rookie sticks) that players use to move the logs on top of one another, trying not to topple over the structure that results from the stacking process.

Chutes and Ladders: A Milton Bradley game first introduced in 1943 for ages three to six, this is a beginner's game requiring no reading. Players move their pieces by the indication of a spinner. Landing on a ladder moves them ahead; dropping down on a chute slides them back.

This game was based on a morality game that came from India by way of Great Britain. In that incarnation, landing on the tail of a snake indicated committing a vice. As punishment, the player had to slide back a space, landing closer to the start position. By landing on a ladder, which indicated a virtue, the player received his or her just recompense by moving ahead. Supposedly the phrase "back to square one" originated with Snakes and Ladders, where an unfortunate throw of the dice could take a player from the top to the bottom. The American version did not incorporate the virtue and vice themes.

Cindy Smart: Toy Quest's early twenty-first century microprocessor-powered, interactive doll with voice-recognition software, Cindy Smart seems to be a high-caliber update of Suzy Smart of the 1960s. The blonde-tressed doll can solve math problems, recognize shapes and colors, respond to preprogrammed questions, and read flash cards in a mostly English language vocabulary (supplemented to a limited extent by German, Spanish, French, and Italian).

circus toys: *See* WOODEN TOYS.

Cissy doll (1955-1964): Introduced by Madame Alexander, this 20- and 21-inch-high doll was one of the first modern fashion icons. Cissy had a mature figure with high-heeled feet. Some dolls could walk. In 1958, Cissette, a smaller version, appeared.

cloth dolls: Cloth was a popular material for homemade playthings, as with rag dolls.

Clue: In 1948, Parker Brothers brought the British game Cluedo to the United States as Clue: The Sherlock Holmes Game. Cluedo is still the Spanish-language version marketed in the United States. Later dropping the subtitle, Clue is a board game of crime detection that investigates the murder of Mr. Boddy in a large house. Players move their pieces around the board as if from room to room. Through a method of questions and deductions, the perpetrator, the weapon, and the scene of the crime are discovered. Among the potential suspects are Colonel Mustard, Mrs. Peacock, and Professor Plum.

A perennial favorite, this most popular whodunit game helped to launch other crime-detecting games mostly based on television shows. Among them were *Dragnet* in 1955, *Perry Mason* in 1959, Philip Marlowe in 1960, the FBI in 1961, all by Transogram, and *77 Sunset Strip* by Lowell in 1959. Clue was the first game to appear as a movie. Earlier collectible versions of the game contain a real (rather than a plastic) rope. A 2000 variant of Clue features *The Simpsons* of the Fox animated series that challenges players to discover who killed Mr. Burns, the television program's evil owner of the Springfield Nuclear Power Plant. The suspects include Homer as Mr. Green, Marge as Mrs. Peacock, and Bart as Professor Plum. Among the six possible weapons are a plutonium rod and a poisoned donut.

Colorforms: Colorforms was invented in 1951 by Harry and Patricia Kislevitz when a friend gave them a roll of flexible vinyl. They first cut out the basic shapes of squares, spheres, rectangles, and triangles, and used them to decorate their bathroom wall. After visiting friends also engaged in the activity, they decided to market it in a large black box (which Patricia pointed out was the preferred method of displaying expensive jewelry).

This activity for ages three and above of stick-on, reusable plastic geometric shapes on a playing board soon morphed into specialty sets. At first there were plastic (instead of paper) doll dress sets. Later designs featured letters and numbers and characters such as Barbie, Mr. Potato Head, Blue's Clues, Barney, and Rugrats. The designer Paul Rand devised the famous Colorforms emblem consisting of a face in a half circle wearing a triangle and resting on a square.

composition dolls: These dolls were blends of wood fiber, paper, and most often sawdust and glue. Their features were often hand painted.

Concentration: Based on the NBC television quiz show that ran from 1958 through 1973 hosted by Hugh Downs, in Concentration two opposing players compete to guess the meaning of a rebus as parts of it are revealed. It was produced by Milton Bradley.

condition: This is a quality that influences the collector, especially important when drawing distinctions between large numbers of mass-produced objects. Although a number of writers and auctioneers in the 1980s attempted to draw up criteria, there is no one agreed-upon standard. Two examples are the following:

> *Hake's Americana and Collectibles* measure
> Mint—flawless, like new
> Near Mint—some wear
> Excellent
> Very Fine
> Fine
> Very Good
> Good
> Fair
> Poor

Lloyd Ralston Toys measure (Ralston was a Connecticut photo engraver who became a coin collector and vendor and later branched out into vintage toy auctions.)

> C10—Mint in the box (a point in the item's favor since a lithographed box is sometimes worth more than the toy itself and contains such useful information as the name and address of manufacturer, copyright, and instructions)
> C9—Mint
> C8—Near mint in the box
> C6—Excellent
> C5—Very fine
> C4—Fine
> C3—Very good
> C2—Good
> Cl—Poor

Connect Four, The Vertical Four-in-a-Row Checkers Game: This is a vertical game of checkers for two players ages seven and up. Introduced in 1974 by Milton Bradley, it was copyrighted in 1998 by Hasbro and is still available. The kit consists of a plastic grid (which contains forty-two checkers in rows of six by seven); two end supports to hold the grid up; twenty-one black checkers and an equal number of red checkers. The object is to be the first to get four like-colored checkers in a horizontal, vertical, or diagonal row. Players take turns dropping checkers one at a time down any of the slots in the top of the grid. In 1989 a small travel version of Connect Four appeared.

Cootie: Cootie is a Milton Bradley game invented by Herb Schaper in 1948 and first commercially produced in 1949. Schaper, an amateur fisherman, was supposedly inspired to make a kids' toy while carving a fishing lure. But, as with other games, there were antecedents to it. In 1934 the name Cootie was used to describe a game in *Leisure* magazine. Nevertheless, Schaper claimed that he gave his game the slang military term for lice. This denotation made some fear that this ex-barber was inspired by encounters during his day job to create the plastic Cootie bug.

Cootie is intended for ages three to seven and is for one to four players. It requires dexterity and patience, but no reading. Throwing a cootie die determines which body part of the bug one picks up. The first to assemble a cootie with a body, head, two eyes, two antennae, six legs, and a tongue wins. There is now a child-friendly version of this game for ages three to six with happy-faced cooties called Cootie Jitterbug.

Corn Popper: Introduced in 1957 by Fisher-Price, the corn popper is best for ages one to three. A child pushes the roller along the floor and watches colorful plastic balls pop against a clear plastic dome, similar to air-popped popcorn. There are myriad other types of push toys, many featuring cartoon characters.

Cracker Jack toys: The caramel-coated popcorn and peanut mix called Cracker Jack was introduced at the 1893 World's Columbian Exposition in Chicago by the local company F.W. Rueckheim. The product did not appear in boxed packages until 1899. Before 1910, Cracker Jack (identified by the logo "Sailor Jack" since 1918) had coupons either on the outside or the inside of the box redeemable for such gifts as jewelry, hats, and utensils. These items accordingly were called "prizes" from 1912 to 1925, "novelties" from 1926 to 1932, and finally, recognizing their then more specific nature, "toys" from 1933 on. Cracker Jack toys are primarily composed of pot metal, aluminum, tin, paper, or, increasingly, plastic. The company's name was changed to Cracker Jack in 1922 and it has been owned by Borden since 1964. Since 1994 the Cracker Jack Collectors Association has conducted conventions and published a newsletter. The Cracker Jack Archives are housed at the Center of Science and Industry in Columbus, Ohio.

Cranium: "The Game for Your Whole Brain" is a board game that challenges players ages twelve and up to whistle, sculpt, draw with their eyes closed, and spell backward. Developed in 1997 by former Microsoft employees Richard Tait and Whit Alexander to allow multiple talents to be displayed, it is sometimes described as a card-based charades game. It debuted in 1998. At least four players are needed for two teams. Activities are organized into four decks:

1. Creative Cat—requests players to make objects out of clay and draw, sometimes while blindfolded
2. Star Performer—asks players to sing, act, or hum
3. Word Worm—asks players to spell, guess word definitions, spell backward, and answer mystery word puzzles in which some letters are missing
4. Data Head—challenges players to answer trivia questions from among true/false and multiple choice responses

In each case, the goal is to be the first team to traverse clockwise around the board and into Cranium Central. The opposing team selects the final challenge.

The items included for play consist of a board, 800 Cranium cards, a ten-sided Cranium die, clay for modeling, a timer, four playing pieces, rules, drawing pads, and pencils. The four decks and the board's quadrants are red, green, blue, and yellow. Active players can add to their game by purchasing Cranium booster boxes with 800 more cards in each set.

As an extension of coffeehouse culture, Cranium was launched in Starbucks. In the summer of 2002, the coffeehouse chain introduced Hear Me Out! This is a game that tests knowledge of pop culture and consumer products and predicts group consensus on selected topics. In the twenty-first century, such ordered pursuits are the contemporary version of the old bar bets.

Crayola crayons: First marketed by the Binney and Smith Company in 1903, a manufacturer of shoe polish, printers' ink, and the inventor of "dustless" chalk, the trademark name Crayola derived from the former teacher Mrs. Alice Binney's coupling of the French word "craie" for chalk with "ola" from the word for oily. Crayons themselves had already been marketed in the nineteenth century by several companies that continued to give Crayola competition, most notably Milton Bradley.

Alice Binney's husband Edwin and his cousin C. Harold Smith's original product, after they took over the Peekskill Chemical Company, contained eight colors (black, blue, brown, green, orange, red, violet, and yellow) in a flip-top green and yellow box. The original targeted clientele consisted of both artists and schoolchildren (hence, nontoxic). Binney and Smith added many more colors in 1949, to a then total of forty-eight. Today, 120 hues are available. The company introduced the sixty-four-crayon container, the first with a built-in sharpener, in 1958 and in 1993 created the Big Box with ninety-six.

There have been only three changes of color names in Crayola history. In 1958, Prussian blue was changed to midnight blue because American children no longer related to German history. In 1962, in a recognition of human diversity, the name flesh was changed to peach. In 1999, Indian red (indicating a tint used in India, but confused with the presumed skin tone of American Indians) became chestnut. But in 1990, in response to children's desires for brighter pigments, Binney and Smith retired eight colors, completely replacing them with bolder shades. The retirees and their replacements (which are not always similar colors) are green blue (now cerulean), raw umber (wild strawberry), orange yellow (jungle green), violet blue (fuchsia), maize (dandelion), lemon yellow (teal blue), blue gray (royal purple), and orange red (vivid tangerine). In 1993, the following appeared: asparagus, cerise, denim, Granny Smith apple, macaroni and cheese, mauvelous, Pacific blue, purple mountain's majesty, razzmatazz, robin's egg blue, shamrock, tickle me pink, timber wolf, tropical rain forest, and wisteria. In 1998, these colors debuted: almond, antique brass, banana mania, beaver, blue bell, brink pink, canary, Caribbean green, cotton candy, cranberry, desert sand, eggplant, fern, fuzzy wuzzy brown, manatee, mountain meadow, outer space, pig pink, pink flamingo, purple heart, shadow, sunset orange, torch red, and vivid violet. Binney and Smith has continued to issue different hues so that few lists purporting to be complete are so for long. With specialty boxes, no one collection contains all current colors.

All of the names of the tints appear on the labels in lower-case letters, for the ease of elementary school pupils, the product's most numerous reading customers. Also, for the youngest customers there are giant My First Crayons. These fit small children's hands more easily and are flat on one side so that they don't roll off the table. Among Crayolas, blue is the most popular color, followed by red, violet, green, carnation pink, black, turquoise blue, blue green, periwinkle, and magenta. Crayola crayons, with their pleasant scent, have proven to be evocative of pleasant childhood memories. Their recognizable odor has been proven to have a soothing effect and to lower blood pressure. Hallmark Cards currently owns the Binney and Smith company.

As a testament to crayons' enduring popularity, Binney and Smith has licensed its trademark to producers of sheets and bedding, backpacks, umbrellas, and wall paints. It also markets color markers, Crayola No Drip Gel Paints, a modeling compound known as Model Magic, color slick crayons, rubber stamps, and colored pencils. It also has sixteen-box specialty crayons. Among these are Construction Paper crayons for use as well on paper bags and cardboard boxes; Pearlite pearly color crayons; Multicolored Glitter crayons and so-called Color Mix-Ups which each have color bursts that produce three different colors. To make worn-down and broken crayons usable (as well as to develop unusual color combinations), in 2002 Crayola introduced a 60-watt, lightbulb-operated, electric-powered Crayola Crayon Maker. Marketed for those eight and up, this melting device put the power of color creating into the consumers' hands.

For the baby boomers (and others who enjoy 1960s and 1970s nostalgia) Crayola in 1999 introduced Retro Colors. This assortment contains colors (all in usual lower-case letters) such as: flower power pink, give peach a chance, platform shoe brown, Woodstock mud brown, cosmic black, shades of black, mellow yellow, tambourine green, psychedelic purple, avocado green, tye-dye lime, bell bottom blue, peace dove white, shag carpet orange, and organic orange. Fluorescent colors had names such as atomic tangerine, blizzard blue, electric lime, hot magenta, laser lemon, magic mint, neon carrot, outrageous orange, radical red, screamin' green, shocking pink, sunglow, and wild watermelon. Coloring is calming and involving for children (for which adults are grateful). The Crayola Hall of Fame (and factory, which is open for tours and for sniffing the aromas of the ingredients paraffin, pigment, and talc) is in Easton, Pennsylvania.

Crazy Bones: Toy Craze, Inc. now of Bedford Heights, Ohio, has marketed this modernized return to the more than 2,000-year-old custom of playing with small pieces of bone. Such ancient pastimes have given rise to games such as jacks and marbles. With Crazy Bones children can play traditional games (like tossing them into the air and getting different scores depending on how they land) by using multicolored bits of skeletal-shaped plastic that also resemble sports or monster figures. One version is shaped like *Toy Story* characters.

Kids only half jokingly are advised to turn grandma's money into Crazy Bones by using her gift money to buy these items. Individual packs can be had for less than $2 but there are also accessories such as cloth bags, collectors' cases, and handbooks. What is old is new again, with contemporary accents. *See* JACKS; MARBLES.

Crazy Soma Cube: Square Root's puzzle for ages seven and up consists of seven different wooden geometric shapes that fit inside a square-shaped 3.5-inch-by-3.5-inch oak tray. The goal is to duplicate the designs in the instruction card. There are nineteen suggested 3-D designs.

Creepy Crawlers: A kit that Mattel first released in 1964 which allowed children to make their own rubbery, wriggly, multicolored bugs from molds, Creepy Crawlers was part of that company's Thingmaker line of Incredible Edibles and Custom Cars. The Creepy Crawler set had the all-important "plasti-goop," as well as a cooling pan, metal molds, and tongs. These last objects were necessary because, unlike the lightbulb-powered Easy-Bake Oven, the Creepy Crawler oven plugged into an electrical outlet and became really hot.

cribbage: A card game played with a standard deck of fifty-two, in cribbage the toy or implement aspect is the scoring board. This is usually made of wood with four rows of thirty holes, two rows for each player. Each contestant has two pegs, either red or black for one player and white for the other. A player marks his or her score (with court cards each counting for ten, the other cards counting their face values) by moving his or her pegs first along the outer row and then back along the inner row. In a round of cards, players mark their score by moving their pegs the appropriate number of holes. For the second score players move their second pegs that number of holes beyond their first peg. The first player to score twelve points (in standard six-card cribbage), that is, to go twice around the board, wins.

D

Darci: Kenner's short-lived blonde, brunette, and red-headed Barbie competitor was introduced in 1978 as a poseable 12.5-inch fashion doll. She was joined by friends Dana and Erica. In 1981 Fashion Fragrance Darci appeared with a requisite miniature bottle of perfume. Collectors like her quality fashions, but Barbie soon became more poseable as well.

dexterity games: Also known as pocket puzzles, handheld games, or palm puzzles, these precursors to the electronic handhelds of the late twentieth century debuted in England around 1840 where they were rolling wooden ball puzzles. Dexterity games are round or square puzzles with marbles or steel ball bearings enclosed by glass or plastic. Players shake or wiggle the pieces to reach the recessed resting places. A challenge to dexterity and eye coordination, the first popular rolling ball puzzle in the United States debuted as Pigs in Clover in 1889.

Among popular themes in these devices were graphics of children's stories, sports, historical events, and later radio, television, and film personalities. Popular before the shopping mall arcades proliferated in the 1970s, these handheld games nearly saturated the American game scene in dime stores and by serving as promotional and giveaway items.

die-cast toys: Lead, the material first used in the nineteenth century for the production of toys shaped in a metal mold under pressure, by the 1930s was replaced by mazac, a magnesium and zinc based alloy. Die-cast toys can be either solid or hollow. Inexpensive, mass-produced objects, such as toy soldiers, were made by pouring molten metal into a mold and letting the excess escape through holes in the top and bottom. In the second decade of the twentieth century, the company Tootsietoy gained fame for miniature toy vehicles and doll furniture made by this process. Other companies famous for die-cast cars were Corgi and Dinky. Currently manufactured popular die-cast products include vehicle lines by Mattel in the well-known Matchbox and Hot Wheels brands.

Disney and Disneyland games: Disneyana first appeared in the early 1930s focused on the premier Disney character Mickey Mouse. Donald Duck and characters related to the studio's first feature-length animated movie *Snow White and the Seven Dwarfs* (1938) soon made their appearance as toy tie-ins. The decade of the 1950s witnessed a profusion of board games related to the opening of Disneyland in 1955 and the popularity of ABC's *The Wonderful World of Disney* program. Both Rand McNally and Transogram released Disneyland games. Whitman's 1955 Mickey Mouse Club Game was set in Disneyland. It focused on Mickey, Minnie, Donald, and others but curiously had no Mouseketeers. Parker Brothers released games based on single "lands": Davy Crockett Frontierland and simply Frontierland in 1955; Adventureland, Fantasyland, and Tomorrowland in 1956. In addition, PB came out with the Disneyland Monorail Game and Riverboat in 1960.

In 1959 Whitman produced the Zorro game based on the Disney television show character who had replaced Davy Crockett. In 1961 it introduced The Wonderful World of Color game based on Disney's television program and in 1965, on its tenth anniversary, produced a new Disneyland game.

Diva Starz: Mattel's 2002 line of "with-it" fashion dolls have the contemporary names Alexa, Miranda, Nikki, Summer, and Tia. All Diva Starz are eleven inches in height. They sport glow-in-the-dark outfits, chunky shoes, and often toy beepers and cell phones. Additional items in the line include Diva Petz—a cat, a dog, and a rabbit. *See* BRATZ DOLLS.

dollhouses: Made commercially in the eighteenth century (although by hand much earlier), nineteenth-century versions of dollhouses were somewhat less elaborate and more likely for children to play with than for adults to view. Usually constructed of wood, dollhouses were later made of metal or plastic. Another material for less expensive versions was lithographed folding cardboard. Renwall made higher quality plastic dollhouse furniture from the 1940s through the 1960s than its competitors Superior, Acme, Ideal, or Marx. Its products had moveable parts such as doors that opened and shelves that could be removed. Dollhouses, complete with human dolls and furnishings, were teaching tools.

dolls: Although many local history museums and historic homes feature dolls and dollhouses, a few museums specialize in dolls. Among these are the following:

The Washington Dolls' House and Toy Museum (founded in 1975 by dollhouse historian Flora Gill Jacobs)
5236 44th Street, NW
Washington, DC 20015

The Doll Museum
520 Thames Street
Newport, Rhode Island 02840

The Fennimore Doll & Toy Museum
1140 Lincoln Avenue
Fennimore, Wisconsin 53809

House of International Dolls
RR #1
Bonshaw, Prince Edward Island, Canada C0A 1C0

The Lois Loftin Doll Museum
120 South Washington Avenue
DeRidder, Louisiana 70734

The Philadelphia Doll Museum
2253 North Broad Street
Philadelphia, Pennsylvania 19132

dominoes: Probably Chinese in origin, dating from the fourteenth century, dominoes are actually flattened dice. Games played with dominoes require both luck and strategy. They spread to the Western world by way of Venice and Naples. The name domino is the term for a long, hooded cloak, worn with a half mask with two eyeholes that resemble the pips on a domino tile. Early sets had one to six pips on each half block without any blank halves. Doubles or spinners are blocks (termed stones or bones, reflecting their original materials) with identical numbers of dots or pips on both ends.

There are numerous domino games but a popular one is double six. Domino tiles begin facedown in a mixed pile from which each player draws five pieces. The player who draws the highest double domino (with the same number on both ends) places that tile in the center. Dominoes are arranged horizontally, except for doubles, which are placed vertically. If no double domino is drawn, all tiles are returned and redrawn. The next player attempts to match one of his or her tiles to the end of the beginning piece. If that player has no match, he or she must take a tile from the draw pile until a match is made. The victor is the first person with no dominoes or the fewest number of spots on any remaining dominoes once all tiles have been drawn.

Dominoes are sometimes stood on edge in long rows. When one is knocked down, the others follow in a mechanical, cascading pattern. Contests are held to construct intricate arrays of tumbling dominoes. This has given rise to the domino theory, attesting to familiarity with dominoes among the general populace. This term was commonly used in the 1950s and 1960s in popular references to American foreign policy fears of one country after another falling to the Communists. This indeed happened in Indochina in the mid-1970s. But a cascading shift in the opposite direction toward democracy took place in Central and Eastern Europe in 1989.

Don't Break the Ice: Introduced more than thirty years ago by Milton Bradley and still available from Hasbro, this is a simple test of strategy and dexterity for two to four players ages three and up. Players, by turn, use plastic red or blue mallets to tap out plastic ice blocks from under a figure of an ice-skating polar bear. There is one large "cube" under the bear and thirty-two smaller plastic cubes. The goal is to keep the bear "skating" or in place as long as possible;

the loser sets the bear tumbling. This is marketed as a good bonding activity for children and adults since it holds the interest of both and involves children who do not yet have reading skills. The game comes with extra cubes so that play can continue in case some of them are lost.

Don't Wake Daddy—The Alarm Clock Game That's Set for Fun: A nonreading game copyrighted by Parker Brothers in 1992 when it was a division of Tonka and now marketed by Hasbro, it is for two to four players ages three to six. Don't Wake Daddy teaches color recognition with twenty-four cards, a spinner, and a game board, and can be used as a togetherness game by children and adults. The youngest player goes first. Players determine how many spaces to advance from a color spinner (which indicates whether one proceeds to the first unoccupied green, red, blue, or yellow space). Participants slip past obstacles such as a cat's tail and roller skates. Spinning a purple star puts the player in front of the leader on the board. If the lead player gets the purple star, he or she spins again. Drawn cards indicate how many times one must press the button on Daddy's alarm clock. Players who "wake" Daddy go all the way back to the beginning. If Daddy sleeps through the alarm, they remain on their space until their next turn. The object is to be the first person to get to the refrigerator at the end of the board before the plastic daddy's alarm goes off and sets him flying out of his bed.

The Dr. Laura Game: Hasbro in 2000 offered a game, based on the radio show host Dr. Laura Schlessinger, which is still available. Aimed at adults, it is for three to six players or teams and is based on actual telephone calls made to her radio program. It presents 600 ethical and moral dilemmas on 300 cards, eighteen voting chips, six pawns to move around a circular game board, and one die. Players roll the six-sided die containing the advice: preach, teach, or nag and guess what Dr. Laura's on-air suggested solutions are to moral quandaries appearing on drawn cards. Participants vote which player gives advice most like the radio guru. The player who comes closest to thinking like Dr. Laura wins. *See* SCRUPLES.

Dr. Seuss Trivia Game: This game by University Games is for two to six players ages six and up, and is based on Seuss's famous rhyming books for kids, although many adults remember them fondly and readily. This company also manufactures two board games with picture cards (with some basic reading required, as one would guess from a Seuss-based product). They are The *Cat in the Hat* Game and The *Green Eggs and Ham* Game, both for two to four players and for ages four and up. Attesting to the continuing resonance of Dr. Seuss in American popular culture is the Dr. Seuss National Memorial Sculpture Garden in Springfield, Massachusetts, where the author was born as Theodor Geisel in 1904. Quite appropriately for someone who did so much to further the cause of reading, the memorial is located next to the local public library. The game was released in 2000.

Easy-Bake Oven: Introduced by Kenner in 1963, this play oven was one of the first girls' toys that actively engaged them. It came equipped with mixes, small baking pans, utensils, a pan pusher, and recipes/instructions. It made baked goods (pretzels, cakes, cookies, brownies, and pizza) with one or two 60-watt lightbulbs powered by batteries (not included). Thus, although it did become hot and could cause burns, the oven used a household object to which most children were daily exposed.

The oven had a very 1960s aquamarine (or turquoise) color. In 1969 an avocado green-hued Premier Oven debuted. A 1978 version was the Easy-Bake Mini-Wave. A current iteration also looks like a microwave oven with a digital time display and uses a 100-watt lightbulb. Topper's Suzy Homemaker imitated the design in 1966 but it is Kenner's that remains (even though an independent Kenner does not). When General Mills ran Kenner for a fifteen-year period from the late 1960s through the early 1980s, it capitalized on this oven by introducing its signature Betty Crocker brand of baked goods products. Hasbro took over Kenner in 1991 and markets this product to both boys and girls, hosting "Baker of the Year" contests for young cooks aged eight to eleven. Hasbro's Queasy Bake Cookerator, introduced in 2002, was marketed especially to boys aged eight to twelve. Using a 100-watt lightbulb, they can make deliberately gross-looking but eatable treats with evocative names such as Mud 'n Crud Cake, Oldy Moldy, Dip 'n Drool Dog Bones, Delicious Dirt, and Bugs'n

Worms. As with the other versions of this oven, the Queasy Bake Cookerator promotes measuring, counting, and cooking skills. Greater emphasis is placed on the process over the product (which admittedly is not of a gourmet caliber). The unique and humorous design of the Cookerator, complete with a brain-shaped warming pan, allows boys to learn the pleasures of cooking without feeling that they are giving up their masculinity.

In 2002 the Easy-Bake line also offered an electric cotton candy maker, a lemonade maker, a blender, and a hand mixer, all for children eight and up.

educational toys: Toys and games have often had didactic aspects to them, whether they taught girls to nurture or sew, boys to compute, or moral lessons (as with the popular menagerie of Noah's Ark). But many modern educational toys were pioneered by toymaker A. C. Gilbert in 1913 (and in 1916 under his own company's moniker). Among them were erector sets (for building metal objects moved by electric motors), chemistry sets, and toy microscopes and telescopes. A great many other toys can fall into this category, however.

electronic games: Electronic games have become increasingly prominent since their initial appearance as bar and arcade entertainment. In 1972, Magnavox debuted Odyssey, the first video game featuring a type of paddle ball. By 1976, electronic versions of squash, hockey, and tennis were available. Pong debuted in 1977 as Ping-Pong played on a computer screen. The Parker Brothers Company early on became involved in producing these games for the home market. In 1977 its first offering in this area was Code Name: Sector. In 1980, it produced Merlin, a hand-held game. In the 1980s Atari games such as Donkey Kong and Pac-Man, a stylized head that ate everything in its path, appeared. Parker Brothers in 1983 premiered Nintendo for home entertainment purposes and in 1986 Nintendo first featured Mario, a now famous game character. In 1989 Nintendo produced Game Boy, a handheld video game. The Parker Brothers division of Hasbro currently sells video versions of some of its classic games, such as Monopoly and Clue. In addition, in 1999 Milton Bradley/ Hasbro introduced electronic handheld versions of Candyland; Connect Four; and Hangman, The Original "Risk Your Neck" Word Guessing Game. The year 2002 witnessed the debut of electronic versions of

Yahtzee from Milton Bradley/Hasbro and UNO from Mattel. *See* THINK-A-TRON.

Elise (1957-1964): A Madame Alexander doll, often an overlooked "middle sister" of fashion dolls, Elise had a hard plastic body with vinyl arms. In 1958, the F.A.O. Schwarz catalog advertised this 16.5-inch doll appropriately as "Sweet 16." However, she was not as fashion conscious as American Character's Sweet Sue Sophisticates.

Ello: Mattel's 2002 construction kit for girls ages six to eight recognizes their wishes to make things as well as their presumed predilection to use toys to explore relationships rather than to compete and dominate. Ello construction toys consist of flat plastic pieces in vibrant colors such as teal, purple, and pink. These pieces are circles, balls, squares, cubes, limbs, flowers, and other shapes that can be joined by special connectors in no preconceived way. This encourages creativity. The materials in Ello-opolis create a town; those in Aquaria result in an underwater scene with fish and mermaids.

Emme: The vinyl Emme doll is the creation of sculptor Robert Tonner and is based on the full-figured model Melissa Miller who, under stage name Emme, hosts the program *Fashion Emergency* on the E! Entertainment Network. The five-feet-eleven-inch, 160 pound, size sixteen real-life Emme agreed to model for the doll provided proceeds went to body image and self-esteem groups. Among the different versions of the doll now offered are: Edgy Emme, Effervescence Emme, Elegance Emme, Energy Emme, Escapade Emme, Ethereal Emme, and Evening Doll Emme. These dolls all come with clothes appropriate to their activities.

Encore: A quiz game unveiled by Endless Games in 1986, Encore is a musical party game for players ages eight and up that tests players' musical memories, specifically song lyrics. It comes with ninety-six cards (each with six clues), a game board, a timer, a die, three pawns, and an instruction book. The challenge is for participants to sing at least six words of a song containing the words listed on a drawn card before the timer runs out.

Erector Set: A. C. Gilbert (a gold-medal Olympic pole vaulter, trained magician, and Yale-educated physician) introduced this metal construction toy for budding engineers in 1913. Gilbert claimed that the inspiration to make the set came to him while observing steel girders designed to switch a railway from steam to electricity along the commuter route from New Haven, Connecticut, to New York City. Gilbert frequently traveled this line to meet with toy buyers for the products of his Mysto magic trick company. He first made girders out of cardboard and then had steel ones constructed.

Gilbert launched perhaps the first major advertising campaign for a toy, targeting fathers and sons in publications such as *Popular Mechanics* and *The Saturday Evening Post*. His come-on phrase was "Hello Boys! Make Lots of Toys." Although not the only metal building kit on the market (Gilbert bought the American rights to Meccano of Great Britain in 1930), his differed in offering motion through motors, gears, and pinions. Gilbert's also had steel beams that were bent at ninety-degree angles. This resulted in a sturdier structure.

In 1916, when he bought out his business partner, Gilbert marketed his products under his own eponymous corporate logo. In 1924, Gilbert vended sets that were kits designed to make only one model such as a truck or locomotive for those who wanted more guidance and less open creativity. His offerings were high-quality, if heavy, items housed in oak cabinets. In 1933, lighter multicolored metal boxes appeared. In the 1950s, these containers were standard red in color and later in that decade (after Gilbert retired in 1954) lower-priced versions debuted in cardboard container canisters.

After Gilbert's death in 1961, cardboard boxes and plastic parts were common. In 1963 brightly colored girders appeared. Sales dropped and the company went out of business in 1967 after the death of Gilbert's son and successor, A. C. Gilbert Jr. Ironically, in 1990, the English-based Meccano bought the license and returned erector sets to the American market. They continue to be more popular among baby boomers (and older generations of men) than among younger boys who are usually attracted to action-packed video entertainment.

Etch A Sketch: Educators view this perennial favorite as an educational toy that develops hand and eye coordination. It was the invention of Paul Chasse, a garage mechanic in Paris. Many toy manufacturers rejected Chasse's "l'écran magique" or magic screen because he asked for too much money for the rights. Eventually, Ohio Art purchased the patent for $25,000 (after having passed on it for less), made a name change and improvements, and began manufacturing the toy in 1960.

Intended for children four and up, it is a drawing device with a classic red-edged gray screen that has two white bottom knobs. One makes vertical lines; the other makes horizontal lines. Together they form diagonal lines which are difficult to control. No doubt it was helped to its popularity by its similarity to a television screen. In contrast to the passivity of television, with Etch A Sketch children can design the scenes. The screen's reverse side is covered by aluminum powder and plastic beads which a metal stylus moved by the knobs dislodges when turned. Shaking the box redistributes the powder and erases the image. A few professional artists (such as Elaine de Kooning) have used this medium to make permanent pictures. The powder can be removed from the Etch A Sketch by drilling holes and spraying a fixative on the back of the screen. This is a step few amateurs take, however.

Famous U.S.A. Landmarks: This educational card game from Learning Resources is for two to four players ages nine and up. The 100 laminated self-checking cards feature questions on U.S. natural parks, monuments, and historical buildings. It also comes with a set of travel stickers. It is still available at select shops.

fantasy items: These objects, currently made for the first time, are intended to appear as if they were originally issued in an earlier time. For example, items debuting in the early twenty-first century might be intended to resemble artifacts from the 1970s. They are usually more popular with adult material culture collectors than with children who want to play rather than accumulate. Fantasy items are not fakes or reproductions because they are not imitations of products made in the earlier era.

fashion dolls: Before the 1950s, these dolls were most often paper in nature. But the first full post–World War II decade saw the appearance of a great many three-dimensional fashion dolls. Although most of these dolls reflected the conservative, highly gender-roled garb of the Eisenhower Era, their existence and popularity indicates that Barbie did not come out of nowhere.

Betsy McCall was a subtle fashion doll that was easier for girls to emulate than her later high-fashion competitor, Barbie. The Ginny doll of *Vogue,* introduced in 1951, was intended for preteens. Madame Alexander dolls such as Cissy and Elise were also pre-Barbie versions of three-dimensional fashion dolls.

Fiddlestix: Toys-N-Things offers a version of the classic Tinkertoys but with some differences. This building set for those ages four and up comes with colorful wooden rods to connect to four different shapes (unlike Tinkertoys' round spools) with holes. Accompanying illustrated instructions are graphic enough for nonreaders to follow them to construct bridges, insects, and endless other objects. Fiddlestix is still available from online retailers.

Finish Lines: Finish Lines is an activity, currently procurable from the company Games For All Reasons for two to four players or teams ages thirteen and up, whose name aptly describes what it challenges participants to do. Based on the information found on any of 500 cards, players strive to complete popular quotations, proverbs, nursery rhymes, catch phases, and musical lyrics. In this game of rapid recognition, the first to complete eleven Finish Lines phrases wins. Players keep track of their wins by collecting tiles and filling up spaces on a game board. Although players may soon have to replay some cards, the interactive aspect of the activity is the main focus, not who prevails.

firefighters: Firemen have often been popular with little boys who eagerly sought to acquire miniature fire trucks or costumes to emulate their heroes. Attesting to the renewed appreciation for firefighters of both genders since September 11, 2001, Hasbro's Milton Bradley line introduced the Firefighter Search & Rescue game in 2002. For two to four players ages six and up, it enjoins all to "Be the hero in this firefighting game." Accordingly, players attempt to extricate all eight members of the Baker family from a conflagration. Each person saved earns one bravery point. Liberating the last member earns the Hero Medal, worth two points. The contestant with the most points wins.

Hasbro that year also introduced the companion Police Chase game for the same age bracket and same number of players. But with the goal to capture a jewel thief by traveling the board all through a hypothetical city and gathering evidence, the heroic aspect of this profession is absent. Lifesaving is more apparent in the third game of this trio, the G.I. Joe Mission: COBRA Headquarters game. In this game each player seeks to upset that evil agency's world domination agenda by seizing its plans.

Fisher-Price toys: As preschool specialists, purveyors of toys for infants and toddlers, Fisher-Price is now part of Mattel. Among its competitors in this demographic group are Playskool and Creative Playthings. *See* FISHER, HOMER G. *in the Toy Inventors chapter.*

Flatsy Dolls: From 1968 until 1971 Ideal made dolls in four different sizes, both male and female, with accessories. Flatsys were like the older-style paper dolls but were made out of thick and durable vinyl. They approached the thickness of Gumby, appearing as though composed of vinyl cut cookie dough. The dolls came with long hair and mod-style outfits. Each Flatsy came on a cardboard liner card with a white plastic clip that attached the doll to the lithographed frame.

Flexible Flyer Sled: This was the invention of the Philadelphia Quaker farm equipment manufacturer Samuel Leeds Allen who in 1889 sought a product to keep his employees on the job when the seasonal demand for his primary product slacked off. After numerous tries, Allen replaced wooden runners with flexible steel, added a moveable, steerable crossbar, a slatted seat, and a trademark red eagle. His sales took off, helped by the then-current interest in wintertime sports such as skating. It is currently made by Finco Sport-n-Toys, Inc., formerly Finney Enterprises, which was established in 1985 by Donald Finney of Canonsburg, Pennsylvania.

Flinch: A card game for ages seven and up by Winning Moves and licensed by Hasbro and known as "the original and still the best stockpile game," Flinch was first published in 1905. The game can be engaged in by two or four in partnerships of two. The first contestant to dispose of all ten numbered cards from his or her stockpile wins. This is done by placing them in numerical order onto the play piles in the center of the table.

Flubber: This commercial tie-in with the "flying rubber" compound (hence the name) in the popular Disney film *The Absent-Minded Professor* (1961) starring Fred MacMurray, caused great problems for Hasbro. After reports that the toy caused a rash in some people, the company dutifully recalled it. After repeated attempts to dispose of it, the ill-fated Flubber ended up being buried in Merrill Hassenfeld's backyard. Hasbro not only survived but learned and flourished.

Four Real: Know It All and Win the Game: This game by University Games is for two or more contestants ages ten and up. Players must answer questions in four parts from among 1,056 in all. They range in difficulty from naming the four seasons to listing the four presidents on Mount Rushmore. In this game that encourages risk, players bid on the right to answer questions arranged in particular categories.

Frisbee: In 1871, William Frisbie established the Frisbie Pie Co. His widow Marian Rose Frisbie baked on until August 1958. According to legend, Yale students tossed the tin pie plates around yelling "Frisbie" to alert those passing by, much like golfers yell "fore." Possibly, they were familiar with this sporting activity of their adult relatives.

The design of the thrown object certainly had antecedents with the ancient Greeks' discus, brought back as a sporting activity a few decades earlier with the revival of the Olympic Games. Ironically for this ancient instrument of play, however, its commercial marketing in the late 1940s was tied to a modern cultural phenomenon. That was the presumed sightings of flying saucers (also known as unidentified flying objects or UFOs) at Roswell, New Mexico, and elsewhere. Walter Frederick Morrison introduced a plastic version of it in 1951 which he dubbed the Pluto Platter. He marketed it first in southern California where, according to some reports, it actually may have been independently invented in the 1940s. Morrison's company, Wham-O (founded in 1948 to make slingshots), spelled it "Frisbee" and it took off with that name. During the 1960s and 1970s, the Frisbee maintained popularity as an alternative to more violent games, and it still has its enthusiasts among kids, adults, and their dog companions.

Frogmen: Baking powder-powered colorful three-inch plastic figures popular in the 1950s, these toys replicated some of the actions of navy frogmen by diving and surfacing in basins of water. They were popular as cereal premiums.

frontier toys: Although cowboy and Indian games have long been popular in the United States, post–World War II radio shows, often transferred to the television screen, revived interest in them. Hopalong Cassidy, The Lone Ranger, and Roy Rogers figured among the personalities that launched many Western toys and games. In 1952 Louis Marx launched the first of his popular play sets (featuring plastic figures, vehicles, and buildings) that were based on a Western theme. This was the Official Roy Rogers Western Town. In time the company made a total of eleven sets inspired by frontier television programs. Among these were *The Life and Legend of Wyatt Earp, The Rifleman,* and *Gunsmoke.*

Davy Crockett-themed raccoon-skin caps, games, toy guns, and lunchboxes proliferated with the three episodes of *Davy Crockett* that Disney aired on ABC-TV from December 1954 through February 1955. Fess Parker as the "king of the wild frontier" inspired boys and girls alike with his motto: "Be sure you're right, then go ahead." A Baltimore court's decision that the name "Davy Crockett" was in the public domain fueled the craze by allowing many manufacturers to turn out products. In the 1960s, before the alternative culture had an influence, Mattel featured a Shoot-n-Shell Winchester rifle. This used Greenie Stickem Caps (individual adhesive cap "rounds") or perforated roll caps (rather than the usual red caps) and safe shells which ejected.

Frosty Sno-Man Sno-Cone Machine: In 1967 Hasbro introduced a plastic machine shaped like a snowman that shaved ice cubes into sno-cones. Equipped with ten different flavor packets, two squeeze bottles, and a shovel, it was as much a toy as a food-producing product. In the 1970s, the popularity of the *Peanuts* comic strip resulted in a Snoopy sno-cone maker. The famously philosophical canine lay in his common pose on top of his doghouse which made sno-cones (which in some regions are termed sno-balls). The latest variation of this product marketed to children (since there are many adult models) was tied in to the Nickelodeon television network's cartoon character SpongeBob SquarePants. It was introduced by Little Kids, Inc. in 2002.

Furbies: "Must-have" toys of the Christmas season of 1998, Hasbro's Tiger Electronics line introduced a battery-operated, interactive five-inch tall character which moved its eyes and ears when it talked, often incessantly. Furby laughs, sneezes, burps, and makes an assortment of other noises. It speaks its own "Furbish" language, while the child who owns it teaches him or her his or her own tongue. A group of Furbies can communicate, a prospect meant to encourage multiple purchases. Toy pets needing active care, Furbies become even crankier if left unattended but do not perish. They proved to be better-liked than their predecessors, Tamagotchis, Japanese electronic toys that needed regular attention lest they die.

FurReal Friends cat: One of Hasbro's hot toys of the 2002 gift-giving holiday season, this mechanical robotic furry cat purrs when petted, hisses when someone pulls its tail, and also meows. Versions of this battery-operated pet include white, black and white, gray, and marmalade (brown and white) cats. Other FurReal Friends come in the form of kittens, puppies, and dogs.

G

The Game of Life: A Milton Bradley perennial favorite and signature game, the company's first offering was the Checkered Game of Life in 1860. Choice and chance determine the outcome. The game is full of the life-cycle events that people experience, such as marriage, births, paydays, and revenge. A spin of the wheel determines where you go next. The game ends when the last player reaches Bankrupt or Millionaire status. Then the player with the most money wins.

Get Real Girl: Julz Chavez, distant cousin of farmworker activist Cesar Chavez, patented this multiracial, action-oriented line of anti-Barbie dolls in 2001. Accompanied by biographies, similar to the historical and more traditional American Girl line (but also reflecting cultural diversity as they do), these dolls, which are still on the market, include Skylar, a Japanese American; Nakia, an African American; and the biracial Gabi. *See* AMERICAN GIRL.

G.I. Joe: Hasbro's best-seller, invented by staff member Don Levine in 1963 (and introduced in 1964) was based on bendable mannequins used in art classes. It may also have been inspired by the short-lived action-adventure television program *The Lieutenant* (1963) although its name relates more to the 1945 film *The Story of G.I. Joe*. The Unique Art Manufacturing Company of Newark, New Jersey, rather obscurely produced a windup tin G.I. Joe and his Bouncing Jeep in the 1940s. G.I. Joe represented all branches of the U.S. military service. He had black, brown, red, or blond hair, often painted on (unlike Barbie's). Joe sported a scar on his right cheek to give him a masculine appeal. But like Mattel's mannequin, Joe had changes of clothing (uniforms) and accessories (weapons and military gear).

Although lead, tin, cast-iron, and small plastic soldiers preceded Joe, his articulated shape was vastly superior. Although boys did make Joe fight, Hasbro offered only fighting men from one side. Girls also wanted to play with Joe and they did not take to a female version geared specifically to them. Like Lionel's pastel train set of the 1950s, the G.I. Joe Nurse, dressed in a Red Cross uniform, became a collectors' item due to its lackluster reception.

G.I. Joe provided a safe outlet for boys who might want to play with their sisters' dolls surreptitiously in the gender-role conscious society of the mid-twentieth century. In 1989, however, the U.S. government officially declared G.I. Joe to be a doll and taxed him at the higher rate that this designation allowed. In some ways, he was the male version of Barbie: an adult-looking mannequin whose clothing reflected different career roles. Accessories for Joe, as with Barbie, were important.

"America's Moveable Fighting Man" who later became "America's Moveable Adventure Man" when an antiwar sentiment set in, G.I. Joe was Hasbro's first "doll" (although he was called an "action figure") and its first item made overseas (in Japan and later Hong Kong). When reintroduced after a hiatus from 1978-1981, he was reduced in height from 11.5 inches (a half inch taller than Barbie) to first eight, then to 3.75 inches because of rising plastic costs. His renewed popularity during the 1980s was attested to by a television series. In 1987 there was also the feature-length *G.I. Joe: The Movie.*

Other Joes came as hunters, astronauts, and ecowarriors, and some had lifelike hair. Before 1991, G.I. Joe accessories proudly did not shoot. But that changed, perhaps in tune with the increasing popularity of violence in films for boys. Perhaps appropriately for a collectible so prized by aging male baby boomers, those early Joes with rooted nylon hair who lost their manes through wear and tear or malicious owners can have them reflocked by professionals. *See* ACTION FIGURES.

Ginny Doll: Ginny Dolls (1948) were created by Jennie Graves for the Vogue Doll Company, named after her daughter Virginia, and carried by the Gimbel's department store. The original reasonably priced dolls had clothing that one could purchase separately. Ginny appeared first as a painted eye doll, then as a sleep-eye doll, and initially as a straight-leg walking doll and later as a bent-knee walker. Because of the decision not to advertise Ginny on television, the doll's sales suffered in comparison to Barbie's. Since 1995, the dolls have become available again from The [Wendy] Lawton Doll Company and are composed of hard plastic like the originals, rather than the later vinyl.

Go to the Head of the Class: In 1936 Milton Bradley minted this game for two to five players for ages seven and up. It consists of a game board, a twenty-eight-page quiz book and instruction manual, playing pieces, and three dice. Players advance from kindergarten to the eighth grade by answering questions in the subjects of language, science, art, music, math, history, literature, and geography. There are three levels of queries: the easiest (for students); intermediate (for scholars); and advanced (for graduates). The game features pop quizzes and homework and the current version available from mail-order houses has contemporary questions. The first person to reach the head of the class and correctly answer a final examination question prevails.

Golliwog dolls: These racially insensitive dolls were especially popular in Great Britain around 1900 that derived from a story for children by Florence Upton, circa 1895. "Adventures of Two Dutch Dolls and a Golliwog" soon led to a popular book series. The Golliwog was a black dandy and minstrel figure dressed in a blue coat and red bow tie, with paws instead of feet and with exaggerated lips and eyes. Milton Bradley used the theme for its Golliwog game of 1907.

gray steel safe: This was a play safe with particular functions. Introduced by Schylling, the safe with red turnstiles had a tray that separated coins from paper money. Some models included a wind-up alarm that the opening of the door triggered. Good for 1950s-style large families, the safe offered a secure place for storing money, diaries, or other valuables away from curious siblings.

Gumby and Pokey: These claymation figures first appeared in Art Clokey's film short *Gumbasia* (1953). They were occasional features on the quintessential 1950s children's program *The Howdy Doody Show*. The green boy Gumby and his orange horse companion Pokey increased their popularity (and marketability) with the debut in 1957 on NBC of *The Gumby Show,* whose long run initially ended in 1967. A pilot had appeared in 1955. These bendable rubber toys were buttressed with interior wires. The Gumby cast on television and in the stores was supplemented by his little sister Minga, his parents, and his pals Prickle the Dinosaur and Goo. Comedian Eddie Murphy rekindled interest among his generation for Gumby with his quirky portrayals of the character in sketches on the baby-boomer classic *Saturday Night Live.* This led to *The All-New Gumby* show and 1995's *Gumby: The Movie. See* BENDIES.

gyroscope: A gyroscope is a precision instrument capable of maintaining the same absolute direction in space despite the movement of the object on which it is balanced. The meaning of the word derives from the Greek for "ring" or "round." It is utilized scientifically to measure equilibrium and to determine direction. Isaac Newton first observed gyroscopic forces in the eighteenth century. Today gyro-controlled directional and navigational systems figure prominently in maritime vessels, aircraft, survey work, and film production. Versions popular among children, available as educational toys since 1917, demonstrate the properties of gyroscopes when balanced on a finger, the tip of a pencil, or a string. The Chandler Company has long made toy gyroscopes. Since 1982, Tedco (the "Toys of Discovery" manufacturer) of Hagerstown, Indiana, has produced them.

H

Hopalong Cassidy: This was the first television program (starring William Boyd as this fictional character) that appeared in the form of a board game (introduced by Milton Bradley in 1950). Curiously enough, it was also the first to be immortalized on a metal lunch box. "Hoppy" items created a precedent for other television programs, especially game shows whose "home versions" were often given away as consolation prizes.

Hot Wheels cars: A Mattel standby of the 1960s and beyond, they were invented by Elliot Handler in 1967 to cash in on the popularity of the miniature metal die-cast cars of the British firm Matchbox. Sizzlers, Mattel's 1970s motorized version of Hot Wheels, were not very successful. Hot Wheels are gravity powered and can reach a speed of 300 mph downhill. Over 700 makes have been created since the first version, a Chevrolet Camaro. The best-selling model is the Chevrolet Corvette. These toys are especially attractive to adult car enthusiasts because of their close resemblance to actual automobiles. They are approximately three inches long and are 1/64th to scale. Real aficionados even look for different hubcap styles and Mattel caters to their needs. Among these styles are sawblade, hot ones, 5-dot, 5-spoke, 3-spoke, lace, fat lace, real riders, 7-spoke, ultra hots, whitewalls, blackwalls, 6-spoke, 8-dot, 8-spoke, and sawblade construction.

How to Succeed in Business Without Really Trying: This was the first stage musical to form the basis for a board game (introduced by Milton Bradley in 1963 before the movie version of 1967). *My Fair Lady* (by Standard Toykraft) soon followed in 1963.

hula hoops: The craze of the year 1958, Wham-O's best-seller, unlike its Frisbee of the previous year, soon dipped in esteem. Of simple and ancient composition, (play hoops stem back to ancient Egypt), the concept was more immediately borrowed from observations made in Australia. The plastic hula hoops could be spun around the waist (and/or feet, arms, neck) while imitating their Hawaiian dance namesake. It could also be thrown into the air and driven along the ground propelled by a skimmer like a traditional wooden hoop. The universality of their appeal to both genders and virtually all age groups accounted for the sale of 25 million hula hoops within several months. Contests were held for enthusiasts to display their levels of expertise. The market was situated by 1959 (but then Hawaii became a state that year, perhaps in part kept in the popular consciousness by the recent fad). There were later reintroductions, including a "shoop-shoop" hula hoop that made this sound when it was used.

I

Ideal's Revlon doll: Called by collectors "Miss Revlon," this vinyl ("lifelike" skin) doll with rooted Saran hair came in several versions. From fifteen to twenty-five inches high, the three most popular Miss Revlons were "Kissing Pink" in a cotton striped dress; "Cherries à la Mode" in a nylon dress; and "Queen of Diamonds" in a velvet evening outfit. Revlon's "Crown Princess" doll of 1955 was a ten-inch tall precursor of this popular line. The Revlon doll of 1957 had pierced ears and feet molded for wearing high heels. To mollify this doll's sophistication, Revlon marketed this doll in a family-friendly way as a big sister to little girls. The advertising for her parent company was obvious in the slogan: "So beautiful her name just had to be Revlon." Toward the end of her run, Revlon dolls were smaller and less expensive, with a bubble-cut hairdo, in the attempt to compete with Barbie.

Imaginiff: Imaginiff, a game invented in Melbourne, Australia, by Andrew and Jack Lawson in 1998 and marketed by Buffalo Games, is intended for three or eight players ages twelve and up. Competitors imagine what their opponents are most similar to, choosing from lists of animals, cars, and the like, and write down their names (or the names of people absent but known to other players) during the game. The goal is more about shocking and provoking laughter than about winning. Players advance in the game if other participants agree that their matches are most accurate.

Innocence Abroad: This Parker Brothers board game was introduced in 1888 to coast on the popularity of Mark Twain's book *The Innocents Abroad*. It was one example of a board game (another was McLoughlin Brothers' 1890 game of Round the World with Nellie Bly) that reflected late nineteenth-century middle-class interest in international travel.

J

jack-in-the-box: A sixteenth-century name for a figure that jumped out of a box, this was once also called a Punch Box because of Jack's resemblance to Punch in the classic puppet show. In the twentieth-century version of the toy, the musical tune played before the jack jumps out is usually "Pop Goes the Weasel." In addition to a harlequin-dressed clown, Curious George or other figures can serve as the jumping jack.

jacks: An ancient game that became a cherished pastime for girls in early twentieth-century America, jacks is played with ten to fourteen small silver or multicolored star-shaped metal pieces and a usually small red rubber ball. Each metal jack consists of four spikes with rounded ends and two with pointed ends. One participant alone or several contestants can play by picking up one or more jacks before the tossed ball either comes to the ground or bounces more than once. Nicknames for variations of the games indicate how many jacks need to be swept up at a time (such as "twosies," "threesies," usually up to "sevensies").

Jacks requires and develops hand-eye coordination and dexterity. Like the game of marbles, late twentieth-century concerns about the safety of very young children around small playing pieces has lessened the presence of this traditional game. Jacks may have originated in Greece as knucklebones because it was played with this part of a sheep's skeleton.

jackstraws: Also called pick-up-sticks, North American settlers and indigenous people developed this game by picking up pieces of straw or wooden splinters by designated color without disturbing the other sticks. This game is usually played using twenty-five sticks in six different colors or six different shades of wood. Players forfeit a turn by moving another stick when retrieving one. Sometimes a black stick is included. The player acquiring this stick can use it to separate two sticks lying together.

Numerous commercial manufacturers readily marketed this easily handmade pastime because there were no copyrights on it. Besides developing hand-eye coordination, jackstraws subliminally taught children that picking things up from a disorganized pile could be satisfying and even fun. One variety makes this more obvious by substituting miniature gardening and farm implements such as rakes, hoes, and shovels for the plain sticks.

Jacob's ladder: This toy has six smooth wooden blocks, joined by a ribbon, that flip by way of double hinges to perform tricks and illusions. This folk toy's name harkens back to the biblical story of a ladder leading up to heaven with angels ascending and descending. It is for ages three and up. A version was also found in King Tut's tomb, perhaps attesting to the Egyptian-Israelite cultural connection. Jacob's ladder is also sometimes called click-clack for the sound that it makes when in motion. The toy can be used to form shapes such as a snake, butterfly, house, flower, and bridge. It can also perform optical illusions, such as appearing to make a penny (or a dollar bill) disappear. Some versions have human figures on the blocks that can appear and disappear depending on how the toy is held. It is currently available from Francis Family Toys in Santa Fe, New Mexico.

Jenga: Jenga, a game advertised as for "edge of your seat" fun, is a stacking toy that can facilitate social interaction at conferences and business meetings. Debuting in the United States in 1987, its name derives from Swahili for "to build." A challenge to players' patience and dexterity, this Milton Bradley product, still available from that division of Hasbro, is for ages eight and up. One or more players remove blocks of alder wood from a stack positioned three across, then deftly put them on top of the structure hoping that it will not collapse. This literal deconstruction exercise for budding architects consists of fifty-four rectangular three-inch wooden blocks. With skill, the structure rises even though riddled with holes. A version using multicolored wooden blocks called Jenga Truth Or Dare uses the same principle of removing wooden blocks without toppling the tower, but these come printed with tricky questions or dares. Among them are describe your most embarrassing moment; say something romantic; and impersonate someone in the room. Not surprisingly, Jenga Truth or Dare is aimed at ages twelve and up. Jenga Xtreme, also for players twelve and up, has more complicated blocks with different angles, which makes the game more difficult.

In 1999, Pavilion, the Toys R Us brand from Geoffrey, Inc., offered Tumbling Tower. This was a variant of Jenga for two or more players ages six and above containing forty-eight wood pieces and a die. Players remove the wooden blocks as the die indicates, not by deciding on their own. In 2002, Mattel introduced UNO Stacko for two to ten players aged seven and above "based on" its UNO card game. The blocks, like those in Jenga, are stacked in groups three across and removed.

Jill (1957): The Vogue Doll Co.'s hard plastic Jill was ten inches tall with high-heeled feet and jointed knees. Jill's friend Jan and Jan's boyfriend Jeff appeared in 1958.

Jotto: Jotto is a word teaser, like Password, by Endless Games for players nine and up, and is advertised as "the original secret word game." It debuted in 1954. Two teams create their own secret five-letter word. Then each side tries to decode the other's shibboleth. Each letter correctly guessed earns a "jot." With few pieces other than two score pads, a holder with rules, and two pencils, Jotto is a good traveling game. Unlike other word-based games such as Scrabble and Yahtzee, there is no need for competitive play to be between intellectual peers.

Ken: Barbie's steady boyfriend, named after Mattel founders Ruth and Elliott Handler's son, is actually two years younger than the fashion queen. Ken Carson (his full name) first appeared in 1961 wearing a red bathing suit, cork sandals, and yellow towel. He has undergone many transformations over the years. The original Ken had either blond or brunette-flocked hair in a crew-cut style. Despite the fact that this haircut meant that there was little hair to begin with, flock-haired Kens often became bald (as did G.I. Joes similarly tressed). The Ken of the following year had painted molded hair and continued with that mode.

In 1965 both Ken and Barbie got bendable legs. He has also had different careers, with the corresponding attire (such as doctor, cowboy, airline pilot, and soda-fountain boy), although not as varied as his consort's. In 1964, Ken got a short-lived best friend, Allan. In 1969, Brad debuted as the boyfriend to Barbie's African-American friend Christie who appeared the previous year. Ken, like Barbie, was available in an edition that talked (for a while, before frequent mechanical failures) from 1968 to 1972. In 1992, a controversial Ken with an earring, bleached-blond hair, and a flashy lavender vest briefly surfaced. This may have been in response to the sensitive, new age males of the 1990s who were sexually ambiguous or metrosexual (that is, straight with a sensitive side). In February 2004, at the same time that Mattel introduced its new Cali (for California) Girl Barbie, it also stated that, after forty-three years, Ken and Barbie were splitting up. The company allowed fans to speculate that the new Mattel male doll Blaine, an Australian boogie boarder, might take Ken's place as Barbie's new beau.

The Kennedys: This is a board game reflecting the cultural significance of a political family. Transco introduced it in 1962 to capitalize on the then-White House family. The inventors, two Harvard students, Jack Winter and Alfred Harrison, invited players to succeed in politics in the television age by cultivating their personal images, gaining support, and avoiding political problems. The game's box featured images of the Kennedys as if chiseled onto Mt. Rushmore. Colorful Products that same year introduced New Frontier, a parody of the Kennedy administration.

Kewpie dolls: These were the invention of magazine writer Rose O'Neill in 1907 who used the little top-knotted figures to illustrate a story for *Ladies' Home Journal*. In 1910, O'Neill authored similar articles for *Women's Home Companion*. The androgenous Kewpie doll (whose term was a variant of cupid) appeared on postcards and as paper dolls before Joseph Kallus, a designer for George Borgfeldt & Company of New York, produced them as celluloid dolls in 1909.

O'Neill applied for a trademark in 1913, but after that several factories in Germany, such as Kestner, turned out bisque versions. After many Kewpies were lost due to Allied torpedoing of German ships during World War I, they were made by the Fulper Pottery Company of New Jersey. As an illustration in magazines, Kewpies helped to sell Jell-O, chocolate, china, and soap.

King Zor: A battery-operated fighting dinosaur offered by Ideal in 1962, this toy included the creature as well as a dart gun, five darts, and five yellow balls that the dinosaur used as projectiles. The object is to hit the lumbering Zor's sensitive disc on his tail to force him to shoot a projectile. Hitting elsewhere loses a dart but does not force him to return fire. The side with the most projectiles left wins. The toy placed a premium on accuracy.

Kismet: A fast-paced word pastime by Endless Games first introduced in 1964, it is like Yahtzee but played with colored dice. Players must match colors as well as words.

kites: These diamond, triangular, square, or rectangular-shaped aerial devices, with or without steadying tails, and attached to their human anchors by strings, originated thousands of years ago in ancient China. They have been made of paper, silk, or linen and more recently plastic. Standard triangular, two-stick kites have bridle lines attached to their ordinarily wooden spines through a hole in the front cover. Cloth tails, sometimes supplemented with cross strips, provide stability in flight. There are also box (cellular "flying crate") kites. These do not have tails.

Since kites were types of aircraft, during the nineteenth century Americans and Europeans experimented with versions capable of carrying human beings either suspended from them or placed within their frames. This conflated the play aspect of kites with the usually more utilitarian element of gliders.

People in Asian countries often craft their kites in the shapes of birds or dragons. In America, Benjamin Franklin was famous for discovering electricity by attaching a key to his kite string and flying it during a storm. Much more recently, American manufacturers have decorated kites with cartoon characters, especially superheroes.

L

Labyrinth: BRIO introduced the original Labyrinth in 1947. It consists of an eleven-inch-by-thirteen-inch wooden box with a maze on top through which one guides a silver-toned ball, guarding so that it does not fall through holes. The game rewards patience and motor skills as players guide the ball through the tricky maze. Small World Toys makes a smaller-sized labyrinth on the same principle for players age five and up. A version of this is still available from Pavilion.

International Playthings has updated Labyrinth with its Maze Mania Game. This is a battery-operated, time-limited (to two minutes), noisy version. It is intended for those ages five to nine who prefer a more action-oriented variation involving going over steps and under arches. In Maze Mania, tilting is necessary in one area to gain enough momentum to slam the ball through a gate in order to open it.

Large Tangram: A tangram is a Chinese puzzle made by cutting a square into five triangles, one square, and one rhomboid. One can form these pieces into thousands of objects such as fish, houses, faces with different expressions, birds, and the like. This artistic puzzle is hundreds of years old and may have originated when someone dropped a tile that broke into these seven geometric shapes. The version offered by Educational Design comes with the seven pieces as well as seventy play cards that illustrate a figure on one side and how it was made on the other. Tangrams challenge the mind and encourage one to see patterns in simple designs.

Leapin' Lizards: This is a brain-teasing game good for travel from Binary Arts Corporation for ages eight and up. The goal is to help five different colored lost lizards find their way home. Paths going around "rocks" on a playing surface indicate the only way that one can go to "leap a lizard." The plastic playing tray contains a storage area for the five plastic lizards and forty challenge cards which vary in difficulty. It is still available.

Lego toys: From the Danish "leg godt" for "play well" (curiously lego means "I put together" in Latin), the carpenter Ole Kirk Christiansen invented Lego building blocks during the 1930s to amuse his children. His son Godtfred turned the wooden bricks to plastic, then to interlocking pieces and initially called them Automatic Binding Bricks. Lego achieved worldwide popularity after first being marketed commercially in 1946. It was sold as complete sets in 1954. Lego blocks are still manufactured in the Danish town of Billund and first became available in the United States in 1961.

The stud-topped bricks, hollow on the bottom, have expanded from the colors red, white, green, yellow, and blue to gray and black. They are now marketed as kits to assemble specific types of buildings. There is a twenty-five-acre Legoland theme park in Billund, Denmark. In addition, in 1999, a similar theme park of 128 acres opened in Carlsbad, California, with over forty rides and adventures. In addition, the California site contains animated replicas of popular tourist areas in the United States such as the Hollywood Bowl, a New England harbor, Mardi Gras in New Orleans, and sites in Washington, DC, all made from Lego bricks.

Lie Detector Game: Mattel's game of "scientific" crime detection for two to four players was first issued in 1960 (with a later reissue as Spy Detector). The game featured twenty-four amusing suspects, one of them guilty of a crime. Players are dealt cards and insert their suspect's card into the lie detector. If a bell sounds, the suspect is lying. Through a process of elimination, suspects are whittled down and the culprit is finally caught.

Lincoln Logs: Similar toys had existed in the nineteenth century. But the architect John Lloyd Wright, son of the famous Frank Lloyd Wright, introduced this system of interlocking, initially redwood beams, either rounded or square and notched on either end, that could be joined to make cabins, forts, and houses. Wright claimed inspiration from the expertly constructed Imperial Hotel in Japan designed by his father. That hotel was one of the few structures to survive the Tokyo Earthquake in 1923.

John Wright achieved marketing success when he launched the product in 1920 by riding the wave of renewed admiration for the sixteenth president after the recent centennial of his birth. Wright advertised his product with the phrase "interesting playthings typifying the spirit of America." The basic wooden beams were later joined by roof gables, doors, and even plastic pieces and human figures. Even greater success for the product (and similar ones such as Halsam's

American Logs) came in the 1950s, capitalizing on the success of the frontier nostalgia and the Davy Crockett television program. The canister sets from that decade are still popular with collectors. The Playskool division of Hasbro once held the Lincoln Log trademark. Currently it is the property of K'Nex, Inc. Another alternative to Lincoln Logs are Roy Toy Building Logs. These were devised by a Maine father of seven with all square-cut pine logs with deep notches to make the buildings sturdier.

Lost in Space: In 1965, *Lost in Space* premiered as a CBS television program (1965-1967) featuring a space family Robinson update on the literary Swiss Family Robinson tale. Paterfamilias professor John Robinson, his wife Maureen, daughters Judy and Penny, and son Will traveled on the spaceship *Jupiter 2* in the attempt to become the first humans to colonize Alpha Centauri. They were accompanied by the Robot, whose directive was to protect the Robinson family, monitoring their environs and providing warnings if danger was imminent. Major Don West piloted the space vehicle. The unexpected presence of Dr. Zachary Smith, a spy, was due to his attempt at sabotaging their mission. He became trapped on board and ultimately was the cause of their becoming "lost in space."

The marketing of many space toys hung on the popularity of this program. Among the offerings was Milton Bradley's *Lost in Space* board game of 1965. Since the game was based on the television pilot, it does not feature Dr. Smith or the Robot. The board displayed a gridlike playing area over the background of a space scene. The box is graphically rich, although the game itself is rather routine. Nevertheless, a feature film of the same name in 1998 made this as well as other associated toys highly desirable by collectors.

Madame Alexander dolls: These elaborate dolls were manufactured by a company founded by Beatrice Behrman in 1923 in the Harlem section of New York City. The first dolls were constructed of rags with pressed, mask-type faces although the costumes were always well made. Later versions were considerably more expensive and sophisticated, aimed at the adult collecting market. In 2001 there were popular culture-inspired dolls based on television's *Laverne and Shirley* and *That Girl* programs.

Madballs: In 1986, AmToy, Inc., a division of the American Greetings Corporation, launched a collection of rubbery balls in deliberately repulsive shapes such as eyeballs and protruding tongues. Both boys and girls found delight with them.

Magic cards: The game Magic: The Gathering, which debuted in 1993, started the modern collectible card game industry. Earlier collectible cards of athletic stars or popular culture images were ordinarily not used to play games but were for trading purposes. Richard Garfield created the game of Magic. The original manufacturer, Wizards of the Coast (now owned by Hasbro), was later famous for producing Pokémon cards, another popular collectible card game. Over 1,000 different cards in virtually endless combinations may be used to play this intricate game that fascinates many adults as well as children. Players become familiar with jargon that applies only to this game.

Two or more contestants engage in Magic by imitating a sorcerers' duel for glory, knowledge, and conquest. They emerge victorious by either damaging their opponents to such an extent that opponents have zero "life points" at the end of a playing round (all begin with twenty); depleting a player's entire deck (called the "library"); or by forcing all opponents to take ten "poison counters." During the game players as sorcerers draw power or "mana" from land cards (swamps, islands, forests, mountains, and plains). Most other cards are "spells," including summons, artifacts, artifact creatures, enchantments, sorceries, instants, and interrupts. "Creatures" are beasts which a player brings to the duel ("summon") and which are used to defend the player. All of the cards are illustrated, and the text on each card describes its specific use.

Each player begins with a custom-built deck of cards of his or her own choosing (with a minimum of sixty cards in the deck). Each person who builds a deck should be sure to include enough land cards as well as additional spells of the types just mentioned. Other accessories needed include one ten- to twenty-sided die; four regular six-sided dice; and a pencil and paper. Play proceeds in a clockwise fashion, with each player going through several stages on his or her turn, until one player emerges victorious.

Since its inception, eight core editions of the game have been released, as well as over thirty expansion sets and several special edition sets. In 2002, Magic Online debuted for Windows users. This interactive version of the game incorporates all of the cards from certain sets and allows individuals to play online matches against one another. A built-in "judge" keeps players from cheating or making illegal plays. When new card sets are released, Magic Online is also updated with the new cards for online use.

Magic 8 Ball: A black plastic ball invented by Abe Bookman of the Alabe Crafts Company in 1946, the Magic 8 Ball gives twenty cryptic answers to questions posed to it. Of these answers, ten are positive, five are negative, and five neutral. The ball's popularity rode the wave of people's interest in predicting the future with Ouija boards, Chinese fortune cookies, and drugstore weight machines.

Magic 8 Ball is a plastic polyhedron with twenty sides with answers that float in a liquid of water, blue coloring, and antifreeze. Many Magic 8 Ball versions are available. The original is a perennial favorite, but there is also one in Spanish, and one that talks (in English). The millennium witnessed the dawn of two additional versions: a pink Magic 8 Ball Date Ball for those aged eight and up and a red Magic 8 Ball Love Ball for those ten and up. The pink ball answers questions like: Will he call? Does he like me? and Will he ask me? The red ball answers relationship questions. They are innocuous (unlike what one might expect): Can my mother come to visit? Can we go to the opera? and Should we buy a new car?

This toy's impact on popular culture is revealed in its frequent appearance on television programs from sitting on Rob Petrie's desk on *The Dick Van Dyke Show,* to its similar placement on Chandler Bing's desk in *Friends,* to being featured on *Murphy Brown, Seinfeld,* and *The Simpsons.* In 1969 Selchow & Righter introduced the board game Behind the "8" Ball. The Magic 8 Ball, in all its diversity and for multiple marketing niches, is currently sold by Mattel.

Magic Rocks: A classic toy marketed at the back of comic books in the 1950s, Magic Rocks, which "grow" in water, debuted in a downtown Los Angeles five-and-ten store in the early 1940s. Brothers James and Arthur Ingoldsby saw the in-store demonstration and by 1945 had formulated their own version which they mass marketed initially as Magic Isle Undersea Garden.

In 1958, the Ingoldsbys, whose main interest was marketing the energy drink Tiger Milk, simplified the name of their toy. The primary ingredients of Magic Rocks are sodium silicate and magnesium sulfate (or Epsom salts). The secret is the dye. Magic Rocks grow an average of two to four inches. An eccentric home decorating accent in the 1950s and 1960s, the comedian Lou Costello had a large black-and-white Magic Rocks garden in his southern California master bedroom.

Magic Slate: This is a quick-erase slate made of black waxed cardboard and a plastic screen. A gentleman in the 1920s invented magic slates and offered the product to R. A. Watkins, the owner of a small commercial printing plant in Aurora, Illinois. The man supposedly handed over his rights to Watkins in return for being bailed out for soliciting an underage girl.

Magic Slates originally were sold to companies who used them in advertising or as premiums (it was a Cracker Jacks prize for a while). Magic Slates often had tic-tac-toe games. During World War II, business took off when the Aurora company made a deal with Disney to market the slates as a child's toy.

Magnetic Puzzle: Frogs, Lizards, and Snakes: Tessellations makes this brainteaser for ages five and up which consists of magnetic pieces resembling frogs, toads, tadpoles, gila monsters, horned lizards, and snakes. One is challenged to put these pieces together into a tessellation, without gaps or overlapping. This was inspired by the optical illusions of the artist M. C. Escher.

mah-jongg: Similar to gin rummy, this Chinese-originated board game became the rage in America during the 1920s. The name is said to mean "sparrow of a hundred intelligences." Like dominoes, which are also of Chinese origin, this social game is often noisily played by slapping the tiles down against each other along a rack or discarding them onto the tabletop. Aficionados fondly recall the sound that the tiles make. Players draw from a pile and try to get a hand of four combinations of three tiles each and a pair of matching tiles. Chinese numbers and symbols cover the 160 ivory (or ivory-colored) tiles. When a player completes his or her hand, he or she halts the play by calling "mah-jongg." This signals that all players must expose their hands for scoring.

Malarky—An Imponderables Bluffing Game: A bluffing game by Patch Products for three to six players ages ten to adult, Malarky gives one player initially the correct answer and the rest make up a response, scoring points when they succeed in getting other players to believe their made-up answers are correct. Pieces consist of 942 questions, six bluff cards, forty-two voting chips, six folders, a die, and a scoring pad. Malarky debuted in 2001 and is still available.

Mancala: An African agricultural game in origin, Mancala is a game of strategy similar to backgammon and Chinese checkers. It is probably the world's oldest game still played and its name derives from the Arabic word for "to move." Traditionally, Mancala boards are carved from wood. Appropriate for players of six years of age and up, it is played with seven pits—six playing pits plus one score pit, the Kalaha—per player. Each of the twelve playing pits contains three seeds (or balls). A player chooses one pit from which to sow the seeds. Each seed in the pit is placed, one at a time, into successive pits, moving counterclockwise around the board. Seeds placed in a player's own Kalaha are his or her pits. He or she must then sow pits in his or her opponent's pit. The game ends when all of the pits on one side of the board are empty. The contestant with the remaining seeds puts them into his or her Kalaha. The winner is the player with the most seeds.

Maptitude: The Game of Global Proportions: This card game for two to four competitors ages ten and up from Resource Games challenges players to draw upon their knowledge of geography (and luck) to rule the world. Using 200 cards (which can be used apart from the game as flash cards), a full-color world map, and fifty scoring tokens, each player attempts to be the first to control one country from all continents (except Antarctica).

marbles: One of the most ancient of childhood games, played with small balls of clay, glass, metal, or composite material, marbles were originally made from bones and fruit pits, then from stones, and played in dirt circles. German handmade beauties were common until machine-made varieties pushed them out in the 1920s. Machine-made varieties are better for shooting since they are uniform. Twentieth-century varieties of marbles include glass swirls; lutz marbles with copper flakes; peppermints with a clear base covered with opaque white glass, often with alternating red and blue bands; micas, transparent glass with flakes of this material; and sulphides, clear glass marbles containing a silvery figure.

Playing marbles consists of rolling, dropping, and knuckling them. A marble being used by a player is sometimes called a taw. Victors usually get to keep (capture) all the marbles when their marble hits an opponent's. Shooting a marble is called knuckling it. "Pee wee" is a common type of marble game, although there are numerous others. His childhood expertise at marbles, not his short stature, gave the legendary baseball player Harold Henry "Pee Wee" Reese his nickname.

Mastermind: A game of strategy from Pressman which debuted in 1971, Mastermind is for two opponents ages eight and up. Each side attempts to make and break secret codes. The game consists of a console with a storage tray, 108 code pegs in six colors, thirty key pegs in two colors, and instructions. Opponents have up to ten tries to guess which color pegs the other side has placed in the console in the form of a hidden code. The code maker supplies the guesser with clues after each successive attempt. Mastermind endeavors to impart the importance of patterns and deductive logic. Possible codes number over 2,000.

Matchbox toys: These are British-made miniature automobiles (as well as other vehicles such as buses, fire engines, and cement mixers), a sideline of the electrical parts firm of Lesney Products, whose toys were first marketed in the early 1950s.

Success with a souvenir version of the newly crowned Queen Elizabeth II's Royal Stage Coach converted the company's interest entirely to die-cast cars.

In 1954, when one of the partners gave his daughter a small matchbox-sized cardboard container to carry a toy to school, the firm received its signature name. Beginning with the mid-1960s, Matchbox found a real competitor in the American-made Hot Wheels of Mattel. The year 2001 saw the introduction of Matchbox Character Cars. At three inches tall, these were made as collectibles for aging baby boomers. The three television icons featured are Bob Denver as Gilligan on the *S S Minnow*; Henry Winkler as the Fonz on a motorcycle; and Barbara Eden as Jeannie in a car. *See* HOT WHEELS CARS.

Mexican jumping beans: These were first marketed in the United States by a candy manufacturer in 1962 who had encountered them on a business trip to Mexico. Sold as a curiosity in groups of three in little plastic boxes, Mexican jumping beans are actually the seed pods of the Yerba de la Flecha tree encasing the eggs of the caterpillar stage of moths. Far away from its home environment, whatever moths actually emerge will not lay eggs or destroy clothing. But their movements inside the pods make the beans jump.

Mille Bornes: Brought to the United States by Parker Brothers in 1962, this is a French automobile, card-based, racing game invented in 1953 by printer of sheet music and road maps Edmond Dujardin. The initial object per game is to play the distance cards to advance your car to the 1,000 km mark (mille bornes) all the while avoiding attacks from your opponent. A game for two, three, four, or six players, it takes its name from kilometer stones showing the distance to the next town. The ultimate goal is to accumulate 5,000 points in several rounds of play. The version sold in the United States bears homage to its French origins by having simple expressions (such as "limite de vitesse" for "speed limit" and "essence" for "gasoline") on the cards in French as well as in English. In this way, it provides some specialized foreign language learning. This car race played with cards provides sedentary, vicarious thrills. Parker Brothers had a popular antecedent to this game called Touring, first produced in 1926.

Mindtrap: A game by Pressman for ages twelve and up, two teams of one or more players answer questions and race along by rolling dice to advance along a score pad. The pad has dark squares forming an optical illusion. The game contains more than 500 riddles and trick questions. But there are a finite number of them in any box (like Trivial Pursuit) unless you buy more from the manufacturer. Mindtrap II with over 400 new cards has Picture It and Shape It categories as well as Brain Cramps and Mystery Cards. Mindtrap is a game that, like Trivial Pursuit, hails from Canada. It was invented by three people in Toronto who, after raising enough capital, introduced it commercially in their own country in 1991. In 1992 Mindtrap debuted in the United States. *See* TRIVIAL PURSUIT.

Misfit toys: These six-inch plush dolls from Stuffins/CVS Pharmacy consist of a cowboy, and a plane, as well as characters from the television specials *Rudolph the Red-Nosed Reindeer* and *Frosty the Snowman*. There are a few twelve-inch versions as well. The name derives from the Island of Misfit Toys, the subject of the *Rudolph* show.

model kits: Although the ships and airplanes of Revell Co. are those most associated with plastic model kits, a great array of these objects also came in ready-to-assemble style. In the late 1940s, Varney introduced the first kit, the Fleet Submarine. Aurora, Revell, and other companies soon offered their own lines of accessories such as plastic cement and paints. Beginning in the 1950s, Aurora produced a collection of monsters in plastic such as Frankenstein, Bride of Frankenstein, Dracula, the Creature from the Black Lagoon, the Wolfman, King Kong, and Dr. Jekyll and Mr. Hyde. In the 1960s this company spoofed these monsters by putting them in dragsters.

Revell, Aurora, AMT, Monogram, Lindberg, MPC, and other kit manufacturers produced the lion's share of flying saucer, Mercury, Gemini, Apollo, and other space program model crafts. AMT was well known for Star Trek models while MPC produced the same for Star Wars. In 1957 Aurora tried to appeal to girls to join the hobby of model building with its line of Guys and Gals of All Nations. Except for the American Indians, all the models had relief maps of their countries on their bases. Unlike toy train manufacturers' appeal to girls with models of their own, these proved to be more successful. Although several scheduled lines, including one of an American bride and groom, were never released, similar models of human figures such as knights, musketeers, and The Beatles (by MPC and Revell) appeared later.

The 1950s introduced educational models of living things as one would see them with X-ray vision. Educational Products, Revell, Pyro, and Skilcraft also made these popular products which were hardly toys (except, perhaps, when the skeletons glowed in the dark). Among these three-dimensional models were the "Visible" dog, man, woman, horse, frog, and pigeon, Chicken Little (which showed how a chicken developed inside an egg), the human heart, skull, and skeleton. Marcel Jovine famously designed Revell's Visible Man and Visible Woman line. Young students, ideally ten and up, could see detailed skeletal, respiratory, digestive, circulatory, and nervous systems.

At about the same time, primarily Aurora produced models of animals as they would appear in the flesh. These included the buffalo, black bear, black fury horse, deer, cougar, and white stallion. Bachmann produced a popular Birds of the World line that were snap-fit in design which meant there was no messy glue to worry about. After assembled one would paint them by number. Bachmann followed up its ornithological line with Dogs of the World. ITC, the Ideal Toy company's hobby division, produced a similar line of dog champions, also to be painted by the number.

Other examples of plastic model kits include: ITC's (1960) line of Marvel Metal animals which could be rubbed so as to impart a metallic effect; Palmer's (1950s) dinosaur skeletons; Multiple Toymakers' (1965) Rube Goldberg kits, such as false teeth extractors and automatic baby feeders; Lindberg's (late 1960s) working clock kits; Revell's amusing Rat Fink and Hawk's Silly Surfers; and Aurora's line of Great Moments in Sport centered on famous athletes. Revell in 2000 sold popular model cars such as the Chrysler P.T. Cruiser and the film character Austin Powers' Shaguar.

Monopoly: Parker Brothers' most famous game was developed in its 1930s form by Charles Darrow, an unemployed heating engineer from Germantown, Pennsylvania. Evidence suggests that there were important antecedents of Monopoly, among them The Landlord's Game. In 1904 Elizabeth Magie Phillips may have attempted to advocate the merits of the economist Henry George's single tax on land through this game. Versions of The Landlord's Game were played in some colleges.

Parker Brothers had turned down Magie Phillips's request for it to be manufactured and marketed in the 1920s, but the company bought her patent the following decade to protect Monopoly, when they finally decided to market that game. This invention of Dan Layman, who had played The Landlord's Game in college, was marketed by the Knapp Electric Company. Finally, an unpublished game intended for the amusement of family and friends called Atlantic City Monopoly, was the invention of that city's Ruthie Thorp Harvey. Darrow may have known of this game through a friend of his wife's.

In any case, the subsequently lauded Darrow presumably remembered happier days at his favorite resort when he developed his game. Parker Brothers initially turned it down in 1934 because of fifty-two "basic errors." It violated several rules of thumb for fun by taking longer than forty-five minutes, having no definite end, and being too complicated for children. Darrow made 5,000 sets of the games of his own and sold them to Wannamaker's Department Store in Philadelphia, and his success changed Parker Brothers' mind. The company bought it in 1935 and made some changes.

This classic real estate trading game for ages eight and up uses the street plan of Atlantic City, New Jersey (although now there are variations), and imparts the vicarious thrill of getting rich. The objective is to become the wealthiest player through buying, renting, and selling property. There are a total of thirty-two houses and twelve hotels and each player is given $1,500 at the beginning. Versions of Monopoly in other countries usually replace Atlantic City real estate with their own and use their own currency. Since 1994, Parker Brothers has licensed USAopoly to create games that reflect various American cities in addition to Atlantic City. Licensed specialty games called Bass Fishing, Bi-Plane, Coca-Cola, Corvette, Golf, Harley-Davidson, Marvel Comics, Mustang, NASCAR, National Parks, Star Trek, and U.S. Space have been developed. In Bass Fishing, prized properties on Lake Castaic, Lake Okeechobee, etc. are for sale; in Golf, prized courses such as Pebble Beach, Pinehurst, PGA West, and the like are available for purchase. Fans of the New York Yankees and the Los Angeles Dodgers can also get collectors' edition sets.

In addition, two Monopoly card games have been developed, distributed by Winning Moves but trademarked by Hasbro, for ages eight and up based on aspects of the classic board game. In Free Parking, which debuted in 1988, players use Feed the Meter cards to add time, then run errands and play Point Cards in order to score. Each errand takes time off the meter. The first player to score 200 points wins. In Waterworks, the first player to complete a leak-free pipeline from his or her valve card to the spout card is the victor. The illustrated cards when placed together form a continuous pipe.

Other, much lesser known, money games include Easy Money by Milton Bradley in 1956 and Big Business by Transogram. This entry from 1959 was popular enough to be issued for almost thirty years. Also in 1959, Hasbro published the *Leave It to Beaver* Money Maker. Milton Bradley's 1962 Square Mile allowed players to be developers on this amount of land. In 1974 the same company marketed Prize Property. Selchow & Righter's entry in 1965 was Go For Broke. Curiously, Parker Brothers itself put out versions of Monopoly with Finance and Fortune in 1936 (in 1947 and in 1958 as well) based on Phillips's 1904 Landlord's Game. Parker Brothers' Payday is an instructional game based on management of a family's finances purporting to show where all the money goes.

In 1966, Selchow & Righter put out an anti-Monopoly of sorts, Komissar, The People's Game. It was anything but an early paradise but comical characters helped players to manage a chuckle during the Cold War 1960s.

In 2003, Hasbro unveiled the Monopoly: *Lord of the Rings* [Movie] Trilogy Edition. Players represented by six tokens standing in for the characters Aragorn, Frodo, Gimli, Galadriel, Gandalf, and Legolas race around the game board to claim territory of Middle Earth. Seven denominations of powers replace Monopoly money. People and Events cards substitute for Chance and Community Chest cards.

Monopoly trivia: In Monopoly, there are forty spaces on the board including avenues named after Atlantic City streets; four railroads (Short Line, B and O, Pennsylvania, and Reading); two utilities (Water Works and the Electric Company); and four chance spaces. There are eight different colors on the board. Marvin Gardens is actually misspelled—it should be Marven Gardens, the only property not named for an Atlantic City street but rather for a nearby community. The Monopoly Man, Rich Uncle Milburn Pennybags, first appeared in 1936. The ten current monopoly tokens are iron, dog, battleship, wheelbarrow, cannon, shoe, race car, horse and rider, thimble, and top hat. All six Monopoly sets on display at the 1959 American National Exhibition in Moscow were stolen. Fidel Castro once ordered all Monopoly sets in Cuba destroyed. The total amount of Monopoly money in a standard game is $15,140. Fifty billion dollars worth of Monopoly money is printed each year—twice as much as the U.S. Mint prints. In 1972, when Atlantic City planned to change the names of its Baltic and Mediterranean Avenues, Monopoly game players protested and the plan was changed.

The end of the twentieth century saw several new versions of the treasured game. In 1999, the standard game got a sack of money as a game piece. A Pokemon edition for ages six to ten contains popular figures such as Pikachu, Bulbasaur, and Charmander as game pieces. Junior Monopoly features amusements along the boardwalk rather than real estate transactions. A Deep Sea Adventure edition allows children to virtually visit places where unique animals thrive. NFL Monopoly allows players to compete to buy any of thirty-one professional football teams and build seating sections and stadiums. Monopoly 2000 provides eight new tokens including a cell phone and a computer. Its dice, houses, and hotels glow.

Mousetrap: A Milton Bradley game for players ages six and up, this Marvin Glass creation was first offered in 1963. A toss of the die tells each player how to build a Rube Goldberg-esqe mechanical mousetrap. The object is to try to catch another player's mouse before he or she captures yours.

Mr. Machine: The creation of the Chicago-based independent toy inventor Marvin Glass, this was an early 1960s wind-up plastic robot by Ideal (topped by an Abe Lincoln-style stovepipe hat). One could view his gears from the outside, take him apart with the plastic wrench supplied, and (presumably) put him together again. Rotating a wheel could make the toy walk in a curve or a circle in addition to in a straight line. The television advertising jingle was happy if incessant:

> Here he comes, here he comes, greatest toy you've ever seen, and his name is—Mr. Machine.
> He is real, he is real, and for you he is ideal, and his name is—Mr. Machine.
> Wind him, go ahead—you can't break the spring [*sic*].
> Take him apart and put him together again.

Mr. Machine soon became the mascot of Ideal Company's television spots in the 1960s, intoning, "It's a wonderful toy—it's Ideal." In 1961, Ideal produced the Mr. Machine Game. The goal was to get him home to his factory. Reintroduced by Ideal in 1978, one could no longer disassemble him. Instead of squawking and ringing a bell, he played a song.

Mr. Potato Head: Invented by George Lerner, a toy inventor from Brooklyn, Hasbro's popular toy was the first ever advertised on local television (in 1952). To add to its allure, this toy was advertised to parents in *Life* magazine. Many of its boxes boasted of this. It took advantage of the fact that kids like to play with their food. The toy consisted of plastic body parts and clothing—small body, shoes, arms, eyes, nose, ears, eyebrows, mustache, and (until 1987) a pipe. Mr. Potato Head (originally called Mr. Potato Head Funny Face Kit) became the paterfamilias of a classic nuclear family in 1953 with the introduction of Mrs. Potato Head and a son Spud and daughter Yam. In 1954, the Spudettes (Potato Head pets) debuted. Later accessories included a car and trailer.

The original Mr. Potato Head had the virtue of transmutability. Children could use different (and real) fruits and vegetables to make each creation a product of their own ingenuity. In 1964, to answer complaints about real vegetables being wasted and lost, the kits changed to include a plastic head to be placed on top of the body (although the first sets had come with a styrofoam head primarily to hold the body pieces together). Supplying plastic heads that did not need sharp body parts also satisified some parental concerns about safety. Also in the 1960s came similar plastic figures that resembled vegetables and fruit, the Tooty Frooty Friends including Pete the Pepper, Oscar the Orange, Cooky the Cucumber, and Katie the Carrot, and Picnic Pals (Franky Frank, Frenchy Fry, Mr. Mustard Head, Willy Burger, Mr. Ketchup Head, and Mrs. Soda Pop Head). In 1984, when Hasbro acquired Playskool, Mr. Potato Head characters began to feature that logo rather than Hasbro's.

With new U.S. safety regulations, the prongs on the face pieces of Mr. Potato Head were made less sharp so that they could not easily pierce real food. The face parts are currently much larger than original (also because of safety rules). Mr. Potato Head has a built-in compartment to store the parts and a baseball cap and sneakers have replaced his derby hat and shoes. In the animated feature film *Toy Story,* Don Rickles, the caustic comedian, provided the voice of Mr. Potato Head, constantly criticizing the actions of other characters. In 2000, Rhode Island commemorated Mr. Potato Head by planting six-foot statues of him around the state.

Muffie dolls: These baby (not adult) fashion dolls were characterized by full lips.

My Little Pony: In 1983 Hasbro introduced small toy horses with manes that can be combed. Market research had previously indicated many girls' near obsession with horses so the toy company capitalized on the phenomenon.

Mystery Date: This was Milton Bradley's beloved and often ridiculed game of romance and surprises. Teenage girls stereotypically long over an ideal date in this game which debuted in 1965. Questions posed in the television commercial include: "Will he be a dream?" (For example, will he be attired in a white tux for the prom or in sports clothes, or a contemporary "dude"?) The box's slogan urges girls to "Meet your secret admirer" while the male voice in the television promotions concluded with "Open the door for your [pause] mystery date" (accompanied by female sighs).

Nancy Ann Storybook Doll: This was a bisque doll based on a 1940s' storybook character, five inches in length, with painted features, jointed arms, and a mohair wig. It was created by Rowena Haskin in 1945 and marketed through Nancy Ann Storybook Dolls, Inc.

Nancy Pearl Action Figure: In 2003, Accoutrements, the parent company of the Archie McPhee novelty store, introduced the Nancy Pearl Action Figure, a take-off on the librarian stereotype. It is modeled on a real Seattle public librarian. This five-inch bespectacled plastic figure, attired in a long dark blue dress, raises its right arm in a shushing gesture when a button on its back is pressed. The doll holds a removable copy of Pearl's latest publication, *Book Lust: Recommended Reading for Every Mood, Moment, and Reason* (2003) and comes with a plastic stack of random books, two bookmarks, and a Nancy Pearl trading card. According to Pearl, "The role of a librarian is to make sense of the world of information. If that's not a qualification for superherodom, what is?"

National Geographic wooden puzzles: This venerable institution dedicated to promoting knowledge of the world contracted with University Games to produce two brainteasers for ages eight and up. Its Great Wall of China Puzzle consists of twelve wooden blocks in different shapes that can be assembled to form two sections of the Great Wall as well as other designs. An instruction sheet offers hints but not the solution. A similar kit contains only seven wooden pieces and a wooden base to form a pyramid. A fact sheet but not the solution to the puzzle accompanies the set.

Nerf ball: A creation of the team of Reyn Guyer, the *Nerf* is a polyurethane ball that was introduced in January 1970. The four-inch ball was sold to Parker Brothers and had the distinct (and very alternative culture hook) of being able to be played without injuring other people or things. It is the "world's official indoor ball," and has no rules. There were larger Super Nerf balls and some people made beds and mobiles out of them. Some people have used them for rehabilitation therapy. The most popular type of Nerf is the football and it is the largest selling football in the world.

nesting dolls: A Russian-inspired method of putting smaller and smaller figures inside larger ones, hand-painted "matryoshka" or nesting dolls currently appear in the form of political figures (initially Russian, now American), often in an amusing fashion.

'NSYNC Backstage Pass Game: Patch's game for two to four fans ages eight and up is a trivia game about the popular boy band "loaded with juicy personal facts." It follows in the footsteps of games revolving around Elvis, the Beatles, the Partridge Family, and Duran Duran. It features the band members: Lance Bass, JC Chasez, Joey Fatone, Chris Kirkpatrick, and Justin Timberlake.

O

Obie: Obie is a deliberately silly-looking pink rubber object from the 1950s, extraterrestrial in appearance. Its eyes, ears, and tongue pop out when it is squeezed. It is primarily a stress reliever but can instruct on how air pressure can build up in a confined area.

Odd Ogg: "Half turtle and half frog" as the television jingle stated, Ideal's 1962 battery-operated creature had no off switch. It came with four colored plastic balls which the player attempted to roll directly below Odd Ogg's tongue. Doing that made him roll forward. Rolling a ball off to the side made him back off and stick his tongue out. The contestant who can bring Odd Ogg closest by rolling the fewest number of balls wins.

old maid: In 1905 Milton Bradley unveiled an illustrated card version (showing a bitter-looking elderly woman in a bonnet, knitting) of a game usually played with a regular deck of cards. The object is not to end up as a spinster. The pejoratively illustrated cards (though later softened by appearing more comical) showed up throughout much of the twentieth century. Possibly, changing social sensibilities and nomenclature made them less marketable. But Cardinal Industries still offered a 1998 version featuring an old maid rather happily knitting away.

On the Edge (handheld balance game): Square Root offers a finished oak box with curvy trails and nooks on the top and a hole at the end to challenge the steadiness and perseverance of players ages seven and up. The object is to coax a steel ball along the trails without letting the ball fall off until it ultimately ends up in the hole.

Operation: This is a Milton Bradley game for players ages six and up. All players are physicians operating on a patient with amusing ailments. "Doctors" try to remove the funny bone, Adam's apple, a wrenched ankle, water on the knee, a charley horse, spare ribs, butterflies in the stomach, and so on. Success earns money; failure causes a battery-operated buzzer to go off (and the patient's red bulb nose to light up). In 2001, Operation Brain Surgery debuted for ages four and up. Doctors reach into an electronic talking head and remove three plastic cranium-related objects (such as a bird brain, a pigheaded condition, a train of thought, an ice cream headache, and an egghead) before the timer goes off and the red nose lights up.

Other games based on hospital situations, such as Transogram's Ben Casey, M.D. of 1961 and Ideal's Dr. Kildare of 1962, showed a much more serious side of medicine. The game Operation was a spin-off of a stunt on the children's television show *Shenanigans*.

Othello: Originally the Game of Annexation (in England) in 1870, then Annex, A Game of Reverses and Reversi (in the United States) in 1888 under the auspices of McLoughlin Brothers Co., Othello made its modern debut in 1976 when Gabriel first marketed it. Othello's modern name derives from Shakespeare's play because of its use of black and white pieces. Pressman currently sells a version for players age eight and up with the slogan "a minute to learn . . . a lifetime to master." Othello is a game of strategy whereby a player tries to outflank his or her opponent.

Ouija: First issued in 1890 by the Kennard Novelty Company, Ouija was purchased by Parker Brothers in 1966. A combination of the French and German words for "yes," two players ages eight and up rest their fingers on the message indicator (a "planchette" or pointer) and let the board spell out the answers, usually to personal questions. On the wooden or increasingly cardboard set are two crescent rows of letters and then a row of numbers. For quick responses, "yes" is written in one corner, "no" is in another, and "good-bye" is at the bottom.

This game undoubtedly initially coasted on the spiritualism sensation of nineteenth-century America. It makes no claims to accuracy and is best played in a group (for emotional support and for entertainment purposes) and on top of two sets of knees (to assist the motion of the pointer). *See* MAGIC 8 BALL.

P

paint-by-numbers kits: These kits for adults and children had their antecedents as far back as the 1920s by crafts companies which used the concept with needlepoint, mosaic, and printmaking products. Picture Craft first introduced and marketed paint-by-numbers kits. The heyday of the idea occurred in the 1950s when the Palmer Paint Company promoted its Craft Master line at the 1951 New York Toy Show. Craft Master had rolled canvas boards and oil paints. The Craftint Corporation introduced acrylic paints. Art Award, Master Artists Materials, Picture Craft, Transogram, Pressman, and Hasbro, as well as Venus Paradise (which also had color pencil-by-the-numbers kits), all competed. Most of the scenes were landscapes, but *The*

Last Supper (a rendition for Palmer Paint by artist Adam Grant, né Grochowski, of the iconic painting) was the most popular religious-themed kit. In 1954 government officials such as J. Edgar Hoover and Nelson Rockefeller hung their paint-by-numbers works in the West Wing of the White House. Craft Master and Art Award also had black (as well as green and gold) velvet painting sets.

Although the kits continued to fascinate craftspeople after the 1950s, they are often cited as emblematic fissures between elite and popular culture in postwar America. They were metaphors for either democratization of art (as indicated by the slogan to sell kits "Every Man a Rembrandt") and a constructive use of new leisure time, or for the mechanization of culture of that decade. Paint-by-numbers' fans are often those who look nostalgically upon that era; their continuing critics are usually those who deride it. Curiously enough, Dan Robbins, the Palmer Paint employee who designed the first paint-by-numbers kit in the 1950s (*Abstract No. One,* actually a still life of fruit in a bowl), based his idea on artist Leonardo Da Vinci's method of assigning numbered portions of paintings to his assistants for completion. Landscapes (especially Paris street scenes) and seascapes and figural designs (such as American Indians and Spanish bullfighters) proved to be much more popular. Craft Master later followed the paint-by-numbers pattern with other kits, such as using crushed marble to make mosaics and painted tile kits.

paper dolls: Paper dolls were first popular among the wealthy classes in Europe and America during the late eighteenth century as cardboard male and female figures with changeable paper costumes. McLoughlin Brothers in the mid-nineteenth century first produced them in large quantities. In the later nineteenth century, versions appeared in magazines such as *Ladies' Home Journal* and *Good Housekeeping* to be cut out and pasted on stiff boards. These mass-produced periodicals made them more widely accessible but less likely to survive over time due to the widespread use of acidic wood pulp fiber after the 1840s. This caused the dolls, like magazines, to become yellow and brittle. Milton Bradley and Selchow & Righter, among other toy manufacturers, produced paper dolls.

Before the introduction of Barbie and other high-fashion icons, paper dolls were an inexpensive way for girls and boys to play dress-up through other characters. Accordingly, they were aspirational figures for young women and men who often could not attire themselves this way themselves (due to their youth or lack of money). The dolls' popularity, owning to their simplicity and low cost, continued throughout the twentieth century. They often featured movie stars, such as Shirley Temple. Traditionally, paper dolls have had foldable tabs on the clothes in order to hang them on the figures. Vinyl variations of paper dolls have included dress-up figures in Colorform sets beginning in the 1950s and the thicker Flatsy dolls of the 1960s. These and magnetic fabric dolls as well as adhesive sticker dolls eliminated the need for tabs.

More recent variations on the classic form of paper doll with tabs have included those based on U.S. Presidential families. Several illustrators became associated with paper dolls in the late twentieth century. Foremost among them is Tom Tierney, who designed for Dover Publications: Ronald Reagan Paper Dolls in Full Color (1984); Lincoln and His Family (1989); Bill Clinton and His Family (1994); and Andrew Jackson and His Family (2001) among others. Tierney designed Dover's series on fashions of the American Family of the 1890s (1987); the American Family of 1900-1920 (1991); the American Family of the 1920s (1988); and the American Family of the 1930s (1991). Also among Tierney's work are Dover's Legendary Baseball Stars Paper Dolls (1985) and his British royalty series. This latter includes the Duke and Duchess of Windsor (1987); Diana, Princess of Wales (1997); and Elizabeth, the Queen Mother (2001). Finally, Tierney designed Ice Skaters Paper Dolls for B. Shackman and Co. (1995). There are other paper doll illustrators for Shackman. Marilyn Henry produced Hollywood celebrity dolls of Claudette Colbert (1994); Joan Crawford (1996); Carmen Miranda (1998); and Barbara Stanwyck (1995) for that company. Karen Prince has illustrated three-dimensional paper dolls that can wear regular dolls' clothes for Hobby House Press (Aimee and Danielle, both in 1996). Brenda Sneathen Mattox has illustrated literary character dolls for Dover such as those from the classics *Pride and Prejudice* (1997) and *The Importance of Being Earnest* (2001).

Finally, to emphasize that the appeal of paper dolls crosses gender lines is the example of A.G. Smith's GI Paper Soldiers for Dover

Publications (1999). This ensemble contains one hundred freestanding World War II–era figures with paper guns, flags, and pup tents.

papier-mâché dolls: Papier-mâché (French for "chewed paper") dolls are made of a rather durable material consisting of paper pulp, paste, and water. They were manufactured in Europe, especially in Germany, as early as the eighteenth century, and in America primarily from 1800 until 1890. Some of these dolls came with wooden limbs or cloth bodies. German immigrant Ludwig Greiner of Philadelphia received his first patent for a cloth-reinforced papier-mâché doll head in 1858 (renewed in 1878). Notably this was probably the first American patent for a doll.

Parcheesi: The game of India, also known as pachisi, is known by an Indian word for twenty-five, which is the highest score that one can get on the dice in the game in one throw. It came via England and first appeared under American commercial auspices when Selchow & Righter marketed it. That company trademarked it in 1874, which was one of the earliest trademarks for an American game.

In this classic race game, each player has four pieces which he or she moves clockwise around the board according to the throw of the dice. After the first piece moves the total number of spaces indicated on the dice, subsequent pieces can follow only if six, ten, or twenty-five is thrown. Players may have one or all four of their players on the board at any one time. If a piece lands on any square other than a distinctively colored "safe from taking" resting space, that piece sends his or her opponent's piece, which is already on that square, back. Although this is called "taking" the piece, it is not actually captured but only sent back home to wait to reenter the contest. Impassable blockades are formed when two pieces of one player occupy a space. From home a pawn can only reenter on a throw of six, ten, or twenty-five. The rival who sent that piece back is allowed another throw. The winner is the first to get all of his or her pieces to the end by a direct throw.

Many game companies have produced versions of Parcheesi under the names of India, Home, Pollyanna, Ludo, and Sorry. More obvious names are Pachisi by Whitman Publishing Co. and Pa-Chiz-Si by Transogram.

Parquetry Blocks 20 Pattern and Puzzle Cards: A Learning Resources puzzle for ages four through seven, this game has no winners or losers. It accentuates cooperation as well as concentration skills and the ability to see patterns. The set consists of thirty-two colorful wooden flat blocks, work tray, and pattern cards. Participants can match the suggestions on the cards or create their own designs. It is currently obtainable.

Pass the Pigs: The "Go Hog-Wild Dice Game" from Winning Moves, as licensed by Hasbro, is available via the Internet and in many toy stores. It is a game of chance with a humorous porcine theme designed by David Moffat in 1977. Two or more players aged seven and up roll two pink plastic piglets and gain or lose points depending on how the figures land. If the piglets are on all fours— a "double trotter"—one gains twenty points. A "snouter" results in ten points. If they lie opposite each other—"pig out"—one gains no points and loses a turn. Various other possibilities consist of an "oinker" (go back to zero); a "leaning jowler" (gain fifteen points); a "razorback" (gain five points); and a "sider" (gain one point). The first to garner 100 points wins. The game contains two "pigs," a scorepad, pencil, and instructions. Small and easy to pack, Pass the Pigs is marketed as a good travel game.

Patti Playpal: Patti Playpal, and her big brother Peter Playpal, were thirty-five-inch-tall companion dolls as large as their child owners. Patti debuted in 1959 with strawberry blonde hair, wearing black Mary Jane shoes and a white pinafore over a gingham dress. In the 1960s this doll was widely available for purchase in supermarkets rather than in toy stores. It is currently being re-created and marketed by Ashton-Drake Galleries.

Pavilion: These toys, made by Geoffrey, Inc. and distributed by Toys "R" Us, feature economical versions of classic games such as chess, checkers, bingo, Chinese checkers, and backgammon.

pedal cars: Metal child-sized versions of automobiles have been around almost as long as the genuine cars. Their existence points to the historic ties between the bicycle and automobile industries since many people in the earlier trade became involved in the latter. Some industrial designers for the adult cars also drew sketches for the Garton tail-finned Kidillac, La Salle, Thunderbolt, and Jet Sweep. Child-sized tractors, locomotives, fire trucks, and nonflying airplanes were rarer than automobiles. By the 1970s, the rising price of steel made the traditional pedal cars too expensive to produce for the general market, although plastic began to replace steel. Among the manufacturers of metal pedal cars are American Machine and Foundry, American National, Eska, ERTL, Garton, Gendron, Murray, and Steelcraft (the last two being the same company producing under different names).

Pente: Meaning five in Greek, the object of Pente is to capture five pairs of your opponent's colored stones or to line up five pairs of your own in a row. The slogan on the box states "easy to learn, yet difficult to master." Pente is mobile—it comes in a red tube and has a vinyl playing board and pouches that carry the playing pieces. It is one of only twenty games recognized in *Game* magazine's hall of fame. A variant of a game played in the Orient centuries ago, Pente became popular in the United States after Pente Games of Stillwater, Oklahoma, revived it in 1977. Parker Brothers purchased it in 1984. In the 1880s Pente was known as Spoils Five. Other monikers include Go, Ninuki-Renju, Go-Moku, and Go-Bang.

Pet Rocks: Pet Rocks debuted in 1975 as the creation of the California advertising man Gary Dahl. Appearing on *The Tonight Show* twice that year, his product became a big seller during that Christmas season. Dahl preferred to use Rosarita Beach Stone for his rocks, included a *Pet Rock Training Manual,* and sold each ensemble for a modest $3.95.

Pez dispensers: A popular cultural icon and one of the most popular, generally low-priced collectibles, the candy Pez (its name derives from the first, middle, and last letter of the German word for peppermint-pfefferminz) was first offered in 1927. But it was sold in tins in Austria for twenty-one years before the fist dispenser, a portable candy machine which allowed one to offer someone a candy without touching it, surfaced in 1948. The early dispensers looked like cigarette lighters since the idea was to get consumers to substitute the candy mints for the smokes. Pez advertisements from the 1940s and 1950s in fact featured a drawing of a cigarette girl in a pillbox hat. Pez received U.S. patent #2,620,061 on October 14, 1949, as a "Pocket Article Dispensing Container." In 1952 a plastic dispenser that handed out a mint from a character head appeared. At that point, Pez dispensers entered the realm of toys. Detailed, full-bodied dispensers from the 1950s included Santa Claus (which, with Mickey Mouse, is one of the best-sellers) and a Space Trooper. Most of the other character dispensers (of which the first licensed was Popeye) were simply character heads atop rectangular cartridge boxes.

Pez has offered over 300 character heads since 1952 (including Tweety Bird, around which an entire episode of the television comedy *Seinfeld* revolved). Vending devices are often based on cartoon or holiday characters. Seasonal offerings include Santa, Snowman, Bunny, Chick, Lamb, Pumpkin Head, Skull, Witch, Valentine Heart (pink), and Valentine Heart (red). Pez makes only two dispensers based on actual people—Betsy Ross and Daniel Boone. Among the top collectibles are "Make-A-Face" dispensers, the wolf-headed dispenser for the 1984 Sarajevo Summer Olympics, and a 1960s creation featuring a miniature baseball bat, ball, and mitt. The 1982 World's Fair dispenser is perhaps the most desirable among collectors since only two are known to exist. Space gun dispensers from the 1950s, which shot out candy, are also quite valuable. The eBay Internet auction site was originally founded in 1995 as Auction Web by Pierre Omidyar to facilitate his wife Pam's Pez dispenser trading. The site's popularity, initially a testament to the desirability of these candy dispensers, and its expansion since that time has made Omidyar a billionaire. With the help of eBay and other sites, the Web has helped create communities of collectors, often geographically widely dispersed.

Pez was produced by Haas Food Manufacturing Corp. (named after its inventor Edward Haas III) until 1973 when it changed its name to Pez Candy, Inc. In that year Pez moved its headquarters to Orange, Connecticut. The dispensers today are made in several countries, including China, Austria, Hungary, and Slovenia. Currently there are five flavors (peppermint, orange, grape [which just replaced cherry], strawberry, and lemon) and sugar-free versions of orange, lemon, and strawberry. Other flavors, such as cola, had been offered, especially in Europe.

Pez dispensers have appeared in films such as *The Client, Stand By Me,* and *E. T.: The Extra-Terrestial.* The "Treat to Eat in a Toy That's Neat" is commemorated in the Burlingame (California) Museum of Pez Memorabilia in the San Francisco Bay area. According to the museum's founder, Gary Doss, Pez is a toy that dispenses candy. What could be better than that?

Pez's success has spawned imitators, such as Fun Flips, a toy that distributes Smarties candies. But Pez itself has rapidly spun off variations of its iconic candy dispensers, such as ballpoint pen dispensers featuring Warner Brothers' Looney Tunes cartoon personages. There are now Pez Petz bubble gum dispensers. Each comes with forty pieces of gum in grape, watermelon, and other fruit flavors. Ten pieces can be stored in a character's stomach at any one time. Set A has the variations of Butler the Penguin, Curly the Pig, Zippy the Dog, and Grinz the Monkey. Set B contains Blubbers the Whale, Sidney the Kangaroo, Purrl the Cat, and Cheeky the Chipmunk. The emblematic Peter Pez (a clown) is currently available as a penlight as well as a car candy dispenser and a mini key chain. Fantasy dispensers comprise a 1970s Yellow Happy Face (never available during that decade) and licensed NFL football-helmeted dispensers. In March 2000, Pez introduced five characters from *The Simpsons* television program. Also, presumably in recognition of the adult market of kids grown old, are the 2002 introduction of Pez Sours in the flavors of pineapple, green apple, watermelon, blue raspberry, and assorted sours. Pez in that year also debuted character-topped Pez fruit-flavored lip balm in orange, strawberry, and grape. For kids (and adult collectors) there was also Pez 100 percent fruit juice in strawberry, grape, sour apple, and sour cherry flavors. Topped with a removable Pez head, this was the product's first edible offering since the candy itself.

pick-up-sticks: *See* JACKSTRAWS.

pinwheels: Pinwheels are colorful devices set into motion by the wind that they catch in curved vanes, made of paper, tinfoil, or plastic, which are mounted on a stick. Similar to whirligigs, they probably were initially handmade. Commercial manufacture began in the early twentieth century. *See* WHIRLIGIGS.

Pit: A game first offered in 1904, Pit is currently available from the Parker Brothers line of Hasbro. It consists of eight suits (of the basic commodities barley, corn, coffee, oranges, oats, soy, sugar, and wheat) of nine cards each, plus a Bull and a Bear card and a corner board. The object is to corner the market on one of the commodities. This happens when a player has all nine cards of the same suit. This teaches stock market strategy to players age seven and up.

Play-Doh: A modeling compound with a pleasant smell of vanilla, Play-Doh was the brainchild of Joe McVicker. Employed in his father's Cincinnati cleaning products firm, McVicker responded to his nursery schoolteacher sister-in-law's request for a malleable clay that would not easily dry out. He formulated a nontoxic compound to clean wallpaper, mailed it off to her school, and then introduced it to the Cincinnati Board of Education. By 1956, the compound was purchased by several major department stores and the family business changed from Kutol Chemical to Rainbow Crafts.

Originally only an off-white color, Play-Doh soon came in blue, pinkish-red, and yellow as well. In the early 1980s, purple, green, orange, and plain pink were added to the line. Hasbro currently manufactures it as part of its Kenner line. In 2003, Target stores unveiled an exclusive product: eight chunky Play-Doh-scented crayons from Hasbro (not Crayola brand) in basic colors in a plastic case for ages three and up.

The Play's the Thing: In 1993 this item debuted, and is still available. A game from Aristoplay for two to four players ages twelve and up, it familiarizes players with parts of Shakespeare's more famous scenes. The regular Master Card set contains excerpts from *Hamlet,* *Julius Caesar,* and *Romeo and Juliet.* Sold separately are a Tragedy Card set (containing *Macbeth, King Lear,* and *Othello*) and a Comedy Card set (with *A Midsummer's Night's Dream, Twelfth Night,* and *As You Like It*). The goal is to "outperform" the other participants by collecting enough cards during the course of the game to act out (optional) a specific scene from a play. As would-be actors in Elizabethan and Jacobean times, players experience stage mix-ups and endure mixed reviews. The game consists of a Master Card set, a Globe Theatre game board, six actor playing pieces, one die, and a booklet with rules, background, and an optional reading list.

pogo sticks: This was initially a brand name for a now generic upright pole with two footrests and a strong spring on the bottom allowing the user to propel himself or herself along the ground by jumping. A pogo stick is similar to stilts. The American traveler George Hansburg presumably discovered the pogo stick in Burma where a father had fashioned a prototype for his barefoot daughter (Pogo) to get to the temple unsullied. Hansburg patented his product in 1919 and Gimbel's Department Store marketed it to great aplomb in the 1920s. Pogo sticks became one of the great crazes of that decade along with yo-yos. Hansburg sold his company, SBI Enterprises, in the 1970s to businessman Irwin Arginsky of Ellenville, New York, and the exercisers have been made continuously since their introduction.

Good for teaching coordination and for losing weight, these jumping devices are like a transportable trampoline for one. One needs to exercise caution, however, in using them only on hard, flat, clean surfaces, not on rock-strewn roads or lawns. *See* ROMPER STOMPERS.

pogs: Drawing on a tradition of milk bottle caps in the nineteenth century which were different, hence, collectible, the name pogs designates the small discs that surfaced in the early 1990s specifically for the purpose of playing a children's game. Initially, their prototypes served the utilitarian purpose of sealing the tops of milk bottles, and later the containers of a brand of Hawaiian juice called POG because of its contents (passion fruit, orange, and guava). Hawaiian children had long played with the caps in a variation of tiddledywinks. By 1994 they spread as a craze to the rest of the United States. There, pogs appeared entirely removed from any practical function; were made of wood, plastic, or metal; and often advertised television series or movies. Frequently they merely bore the images of action heroes or fanciful characters. The passion for collecting pogs did not last beyond that decade, however. *See* TIDDLYWINKS.

Pokémon: Also known as "Pocket Monsters," Pokémon are the invention of Japanese entrepreneur Satoshi Tajiri, who thought up a universe inhabited by trainable monsters. Children catch and instruct these mini monsters and use them as guardians and companions to catch and challenge other pocket monsters. Their human friends can earn badges and become Pokémon masters. With 151 initially (but with an expanding universe), Pokémon characters have different powers. They can evolve into other, more powerful characters, changing their names slightly.

The most popular characters are the yellow mouse mascot, Pikachu, (whose tail can shoot out lightning bolts when in combat), the first one the boy character, Ash, caught; Charmander, a dragon salamander-like creature with fire emanating from its tail; and Squirtle, a turtle. Some Pokémons are benevolent; others are sinister. They cannot be killed, only knocked unconscious. As cuddly characters whose activities are relatively nonviolent, by late twentieth-century standards, they appeal to both boys and girls. This always broadens their market appeal. The plot of the original story revolved around the boy hero Ash Ketchum and his nemesis Gary. In addition to Ash, other human characters include Misty and Brock.

In 1998, Pokémon first immigrated to the United States. It had made its appearance in its home country as a handheld Nintendo Game Boy game, then as a television program, and finally in trading cards, backpacks, T-shirts, and other commercial products. Pokémon characters impart autonomy to children (from parents, but not from marketers). Their relatively inexpensive price and multiplicity of characters lend to their value as collectibles among children. In November 1999, Pokémon appeared in a motion picture (which was advertised as its first film). Hasbro purchased Wizards of the Coast, the Seattle-based manufacturer of the Pokémon trading card game, in 1999.

Potholder Loom: Harrisville Designs is one of the vendors for the traditional metal potholder loom that comes with different colored cotton loops, a plastic hook, a seven-inch square metal loom, and simple instructions. Another company, Craft House, offers a plastic version of the loom. Children ages seven and up develop hand-eye coordination, patience, and dexterity. They experience recurring satisfaction when they see adults using the items that they made.

Pound Puppies: Mike Bowling left a Cincinnati automobile factory to promote his invention, Pound Puppies. He designed them in 1984 and they were released the same year. Tonka soon bought him out. A canine version of Cabbage Patch Kids dolls, Pound Puppies undoubtedly rode on their fame. Children adopted them (as well as members of the cat version, Pound Pur-r-ries, beginning in 1986). Pound Puppies had an animated television series (similar to the Strawberry Shortcake dolls) and children often accumulated large numbers of them, like the earlier Care Bears and the subsequent Beanie Babies. *See also* BEANIE BABIES; CABBAGE PATCH KIDS DOLLS.

Power Rangers, Mighty Morphin: These characters appear in a FOX television program with a toy tie-in. They are violent but teach teamwork, environmental concerns, and the importance of diversity. A film about this crime-fighting team debuted in 1995 as *Mighty Morphin Power Rangers: The Movie*. *See* ACTION FIGURES.

pull toys: This category of playthings for toddlers has long been commercially dominated by Fisher-Price, although the origin of pull toys dates back to ancient Egypt. Small wooden horses or other animals were popular in the nineteenth century. The following century, Donald Duck and the Pony Chime became favorite designs. One popular 1950s pull toy, incorporating a Slinky in its midsection, was Slinky Dog.

pull-string talking toys: Chatty Cathy was most prominent among pull-string talking toys although even Barbie and her friends appeared in conversational editions in the late 1960s and early 1970s. *See* TALKING DOLLS.

puppets: Puppets are small-scale figures of human beings or other animate objects appropriately painted and costumed. They are moved by human, not mechanical, means either by a hand or by a rod (from below) or by wires or strings (from above). Used as a means of communication and performance art, puppets date to ancient Greece, China, and India. There are several main types of these playthings:

1. Hand or glove: these have a hollow cloth body that fits over a hand; there are normally no legs. These were the traditional puppets of medieval Europe.
2. Marionette (string): full-length figures that are ordinarily moved by at least nine threads, connecting both legs, both hands, both shoulders, both ears, and the base of the spine. These can be very sophisticated and can represent almost every animal or human gesture.
3. Rod: these are the traditional puppets of the Indonesian islands of Java and Bali.

Puppets used in television programs aimed primarily, but not exclusively, at children often were replicated and marketed as toys. In 1947 in the United States, Burr Tillstrom began his television career with Kukla, a small boy, Ollie, a dragon, and assorted other characters who were hand puppets. In the late 1940s and throughout the 1950s the eponymous *Howdy Doody Show* featured a cast of marionettes. Soupy Sales had the large hand puppets White Fang and Black Tooth. In 1969, Jim Henson introduced the Muppets on the educational program *Sesame Street*. As their name indicates, Muppets combined the qualities of hand puppets and marionettes. Muppets moved from television to the big screen (much as some of their human counterparts did) in a series of films beginning with *The Muppet Movie* in 1979. Caricatures of British politicians were lampooned in the series *Spitting Image* (running 1984-1992). This program briefly traversed the Atlantic to feature American politicos. Puppets deliberately constructed to strike blows with boxing gloves appeared in the 1980s. Among the more popular versions were those of the television star Mr. T, President Ronald Reagan, and a generic, traditionally habited nun.

push toys: This is a plaything designed to be propelled by a metal, wooden, or plastic extension, usually wielded by a toddler. It usually has colorful moving parts that make sounds when the device is pushed along. The extension provides support for a child beginning to walk; the sound and color generate interest. Examples of push toys include child-size lawn mowers, shopping carts, wooden ducks, and other birds. *See* CORN POPPER; PULL TOYS.

puzzles: Puzzles can be word-based brainteasers, mazes, or cut up pieces to be assembled to form a picture. They are items manufactured for the purpose of play that requires a solution. The first authenticated jigsaw puzzle was the product of John Spilsbury, a London mapmaker of the early 1760s. American toy manufacturers such as S. B. Ives and the McLoughlin Brothers began offering puzzles before the Civil War. There were several periods of jigsaw puzzle crazes: the 1880s-1890s, 1908-1909, and 1932-1933. More resilient and expensive wooden puzzles prevailed before the 1920s with die-cut cardboard puzzles largely taking their place except among collecting aficionados. Jigsaw puzzles experienced revivals during World War II and in the mid-1960s with Springbok puzzles.

Early puzzles for children featured historical personages and other pedagogical themes. That was surpassed by cartoon and literary characters. Adults have generally preferred more challenging teasers, especially the handmade wooden puzzles (as opposed to mass-produced, cardboard items) that either interlock or do not, are cut on color lines, and include false corners, open spaces in the center, and nonrectangular borders. Advertisers often offered puzzles in return for purchasing their products. They either were scenes not related to their product or those that boldly trumpeted the product itself.

Toy giant Hasbro put a new spin on puzzles with its late 1990s foam-backed 3D puzzle series. Among these are another permutation of Monopoly in the form of a puzzle called Build It—Then Play It as well as a replica of the *Titanic,* a teepee, a fire engine, and an old-fashioned red British telephone booth.

Mechanical puzzles consist of metal disentanglement challenges, sliding blocks (a form of sequential movement) puzzles, dexterity puzzles, vanish puzzles, impossible object puzzles, and folding puzzles. Recently, companies such as Binary Arts have fashioned well-made puzzles to challenge the skills of players of different ages and levels of skill. See these individual puzzles under their respective names.

Q

Quick Pix: This is a series of flash card games from Aristoplay which allows young people to learn while interacting and competing. Quick Pix: Not Just a Geography Game is a 1999 travel card game for ages seven and up for two to six participants. It challenges players to be the first to match five countries to their correct regions. Quick Pix: Not Just a Math Game asks players to learn sums and differences between the numbers one through eighteen. Quick Pix: Not Just an Animal Game helps children learn which animals belong to which larger groups. Also in the series are Not Just a Multiplication Game and Not Just a Money Game.

R

Rack-O: This game of skill and luck was introduced by Parker Brothers. It is currently under Hasbro's copyright (1992), and there were editions in 1978 and 1987 as well. Two to four players ages eight and up put their cards in their racks in each round so that numbers (from one to sixty) read in any numerical progression from a low number at the front to a high number at the back. Each player is initially dealt ten cards. Undistributed cards are placed number-side down to form a Draw Pile. The top card is then turned face up to make the Discard Pile. Each player successively takes the top card from either pile. If taken from the visible Discard Pile, he or she must exchange the card with one from the player's set. If selected from the Draw Pile, the player may exchange it for a card or may choose to reject it. The round ends when a player gets all ten of his or her cards in order. Play continues until one player achieves 500 points.

Radio Flyer Wagon: A metal wagon first fashioned by Italian immigrant Antonio Pasin, the Radio Flyer was preceded in 1917 by a wooden wagon fashioned by the same craftsman. By 1923 he called his then metal, mass-produced wagons "Liberty Coasters." The words "Radio Flyer," which are still stenciled by hand, both honor the invention of another Italian and connote speed. Pasin heavily promoted his product at the 1933-1934 Chicago World's Fair. Variations include the Streak-O-Lite of 1934, with control dials and working headlights; the Radio Rancher of 1957, with high sides; and a 1995 All Terrain Wagon. The 1992 feature film *Radio Flyer* paid homage to this icon of childhood which was used for racing as well as making newspaper deliveries.

Raggedy Ann: This doll originated with a restuffed and repainted rag doll that a young girl, Marcella Gruelle, found in her grandmother's attic in 1906. Her father, Connecticut-based artist and political cartoonist Johnny Gruelle (1880-1938), developed stories about the doll. The name derived from a composite of two poems by family friend James Whitcomb Riley, "Little Orphan Annie" and "The Raggedy Man." In 1915 Gruelle copyrighted the name and began making a small number of handcrafted dolls with brown rather than the later, more enduring red yarn hair.

About that time, Marcella became fatally ill from a smallpox vaccination gone wrong. In tribute to her, Gruelle wrote and illustrated a compilation of the stories in 1918 that he had told Marcella over the years. In that year the Volland Company began commercially manufacturing a Raggedy Ann doll. Until his death, Gruelle wrote and illustrated an average of one Raggedy Ann and Andy story a year.

In 1920, Gruelle first offered the doll for sale at Marshall Field's Department Store in Chicago. That was the year of Ann's friend Raggedy Andy's copyright. The freckle-faced doll, then with red yarn hair, a triangle-shaped nose, red-striped legs, and shoe-button eyes, had a silk-screened heart with "I love you" on its chest. Gruelle's original homemade dolls may have had candy hearts sewn within them. The Volland variation had a cardboard heart. Later manufactured by Knickerbocker Toys, Tonka took the concession over and Hasbro began producing Raggedy Ann when it in turn absorbed Tonka. Due to its cuddly appearance and nostalgic resonances, the doll still finds a ready market today. The Johnny Gruelle, Raggedy Ann and Andy Museum opened in the artist's birthplace of Arcola, Illinois, in 1999.

ramp walkers: Also known as incline walkers, walking toys, slant walkers, or table walkers, these character pieces saunter down an inclined board solely by means of gravity. First appearing in the United States in the 1870s, perhaps as a cast-iron elephant walker, Marx, Milton Bradley, and many other toy companies in the twentieth century manufactured them in plastic. In the guise of animals, sport figures, or cartoon characters, ramp walkers were often cereal premiums, promotional giveaways, or dime-store staples. Some came with their own incline boards or with weight and string attachments to suspend from front loops.

religious toys: Although early-nineteenth-century games were constructed to deliver moral messages, deliberately religious toys in the

United States of the twentieth century were rare and rather unsuccessful. No matter how noble the concept, Ideal's Baby Jesus of 1958 doll was a marketing failure. But with the revival of faith-based values in the early twenty-first century, such developmental tools have become more common. Game and puzzle company Talicor offered the BibleMan board game. Players combat villains using the virtues of Faith, Love, Truth, Joy, Patience, and Forgiveness in order to rescue children who have been tricked by God's enemies. The first to deliver the six children to the town church wins.

CatholicChild.com offers My Mass Tote which includes coloring books, a picture missal, and Noah's Ark Lace'n Trace to busy children while in church. Prayer Bears from the same company play prayers when their stomachs are pressed. Astrolabe Islamic Media sells an interactive Arabic Talking School Bus that teaches the Arabic alphabet. *See* CARE BEARS *under* TEDDY BEARS.

Reversi: *See* OTHELLO.

riding toys: Rocking or hobbyhorses have been popular since the seventeenth century. Germany was renown for carved horses on curved rockers. A nineteenth-century variant featured a horse mounted on a tricycle.

Ripley's Believe It or Not! Game: This is University Games's offering based on the early twentieth-century newspaper feature by Robert Ripley. The original feature, usually running on the comic strip page of newspapers, led to the establishment of several museums showcasing oddities often thought too unusual to be true. In this board game, two or more players ages eight and up listen to a wild "fact" in the form of a question which may or may not be true. A total of 880 questions are inscribed on 220 cards. Players collect tickets for a Believe It or Not! Museum if they correctly assess whether a fact is true or not. Tickets are good for exhibit cards (there are 110 of these in the game). The winner is the player who gets to open a museum.

Risk, the Game of Global Domination: Originating in France and debuting in the United States in 1959, Hasbro's Risk is intended for two to six players ages ten and up. It is played with 360 military miniatures between two power systems ranged on a Mercator-style map of the world. In 2003, Hasbro introduced the *Lord of the Rings*

[Movie] Trilogy Edition for two to four players ages nine and up. In it, the evil Mordor side engages the benevolent Gondor side in the battle for Middle-earth.

Robby (Robert) the Robot: "The mechanical man," as the television jingle proclaimed, this Ideal toy was based on the character in the 1956 Disney science fiction film *Forbidden Planet*. A Japanese-manufactured product in the late 1950s, new wind-up versions appeared in 2000 to satisfy the desires of nostalgic baby boomers. Unlike earlier toy robots, this one was plastic, the "new" toy material, instead of metal. Children could move its arms and flash its lights by using remote controls.

Rock'Em Sock'Em Robots: Introduced by Marx in 1966, this toy presented a particularly violent form of boxing as fun through the ruse of the fighters being robots rather than human figures. Red Rocker, at 375 pounds, from Soltarus II faced off the Blue Bomber, from Umgluck, at 382 pounds. When punches connected, the opposing robot's head rose up.

rock 'n roll games: Among offerings with the theme of rock'n roll are: The Beatles' Flip Your Wig Game (Milton Bradley, 1964); Chubby Checker's Limbo Game (Wham-O, 1961); Duran Duran (Milton Bradley, 1985); Elvis (Boxcar Enterprises, 1978); Elvis Presley (Teenage Games, 1957); Hullabaloo Electric Teen Game (Remco, 1965) and Shindig (Remco, 1965), both based on television music programs; the Monkees Game, Hey! Hey! (Transogram, 1967); and the Partridge Family Game (Milton Bradley, 1971).

roly-poly: These are balance toys in clown or cartoon characters with large rounded, usually sand-weighted bottoms that were popular throughout the twentieth century. A. Schoenhut Company of Philadelphia marketed early versions. Small roly-polys can be pushed over. Larger ones bop up when punched.

Romper Stompers: Hasbro introduced these plastic cups connected to steadying, adjustable, handheld plastic ropes in 1975 as part of its Romper Room line (tied into the children's television program of the same name). Somewhat similar to stilts, but not as tall and with ropes rather than poles, Romper Stompers undoubtedly taught children the importance of balance and imparted to them the empowering sensation of being tall.

Rook: Debuting in 1906, Rook is a card game now manufactured by the Parker Brothers Division of Hasbro. It has many variations, one of the most popular being Kentucky Discard in which the object is to score 300 points. Rook is popular among those who find using standard playing cards morally offensive.

Rubik's Bricks: A game of logic for single players ages eight and up by Oddzon, this is a three-dimensional toy for thinkers, a variation on Soma Cube but with two colors instead of just one. Nine bricks are on each side and there are 880 ways of making a cube.

Rubik's Cube: This sensation of the 1980s is a multicolored, hand-held puzzle invented in 1975 by Erno Rubik, a Hungarian engineer. It was first marketed in 1977 and was a best-seller from 1980-1983, making Rubik the first self-made millionaire in what was then the Communist Bloc. The structural design consists of twenty-six individual cubes making up a big cube which is the toy. Each layer of nine cubes can twist and the layers overlap. The goal is to realign all six sides according to color in the shortest time and with the fewest possible moves. The fastest speed recorded was about twenty-two seconds. No one has solved the puzzle in less than fifty-two moves, although twenty-two moves is considered possible.

An American, Larry Nichols, actually patented his cube before Rubik. But toy companies rejected it (including Ideal, which later bought the rights to Rubik's cube). Nichols's model was held together by magnets, unlike Rubik's. At the height of the cube's popularity, enthusiasts or "Cubic Rubes" formed clubs, especially at places such as MIT. Square 1, a variation of the game that appeared at the end of the 1990s, starts out flat but then twists into a three-dimensional shape.

Rubik's Snakes: A great office toy from the 1980s, Rubik's Snakes by Oddzon is for ages eight and up. One can change the shape of the object by twisting it into animals or other things. There is no wrong answer.

Rummikub: A family, gin-rummy-type game distributed in the United States since 1997 by Pressman, Rummikub is intended for two to four players ages eight and up. Playing equipment consists of 104 engraved tiles numbered one to thirteen in four colors (black, orange, red, and blue); two joker tiles; four racks to hold the tiles; and instructions. The object is to be the first to get all tiles from the rack onto the table. Play proceeds clockwise—every player takes fourteen tiles and arranges them into runs or groups on his or her rack. The remaining tiles go into the pool.

A group is a set of either three or four tiles of the same number but in different colors. A run is a set of three or more consecutive numbers all of the same color. The game continues until a player empties his or her rack and calls out, "Rummikub!" The other players then add up the points on their racks. The winner of the round receives a positive score equal to the total of all the losers' points. At the end of a session, each player adds his or her minus and plus scores. The player with the highest score is the overall winner. The plus scores should equal the total of the minus scores in each round and in the final tally.

Ephraim Hertzano developed Rummikub in the early 1930s. At the end of the twentieth century, it was the third best-selling game in the world and Israel's number-one export game (from Lemada Light Industries, Ltd). Based on numbers, it overcomes language barriers. Without images of kings and queens, it is not banned by any religion or political regime. Hollywood personalities Elizabeth Taylor, Telly Savalas, Don Rickles, and Bob Newhart have claimed it as their favorite game.

Rush Hour: In this sliding, three-dimensional block puzzle for ages eight and up from Binary Arts that challenges sequential thinking, a player's red car must weave through four levels of difficult traffic jams. As with many late-twentieth-century games, this one conveniently contains a storage compartment. Puzzle cards contain step-by-step solutions. Like a crossword puzzle without words, this icon-like puzzler is made for the computer age. Among its assets are that it is geared to different skill levels and it is compact enough to serve as a travel game.

Rush Hour 2 offers forty new challenge cards and a new red convertible. Rush Hour 3 is an add-on accessory package with forty more Rush Hour cards and with a toy white stretch limousine. Rush Hour

Junior, for ages six to eight, like Monopoly Junior, is at an elementary level with a child's theme and perspective. Here the goal is to maneuver a little white ice cream truck home before its cargo melts. There are still different levels of play. It includes sixteen multihued vehicles, forty color-coded cards, instructions, and a solution booklet. Safari Rush Hour, for ages six and up, set on an African savannah, challenges players to maneuver around animal-themed obstacles.

S

sand toys: These beach toys include pails, shovels, and watering cans, and sometimes water pumps, all originally made of pressed metal. In 1879, Jesse Crandall introduced a Sandometer beach toy. Wolverine Supply & Mfg. Co. marketed Sandy Andy and its Automatic Sand Crane while Ohio Art had a Sand Lift. During the 1920s Julius Chein and Company of New York City popularized its version of often colorfully painted beach tin toys which sift sand by use of gravity. The child either did the sifting manually with a sieve or watched a more complex toy do so. Many of these devices were inspired by the carnival atmosphere of nearby Coney Island. Marketed primarily through the F. W. Woolworth Co., these toys had to be redesigned in the 1960s so as to conform with new laws banning sharp metal edges. Tin toys largely disappeared, as did the reorganized Atlantic Cheinco in 1992 (and Woolworth's itself).

Saralee: This eponymous black doll produced by Ideal for the commercial market in 1953 was a pioneer when it appeared. Realistic-looking dolls resembling people of color were uncommon and scarcer still were black dolls which were not simply variations of white dolls. Because of their rarity, black dolls are usually more valuable than their white counterparts. This doll, measuring seventeen inches, decked out in yellow and white organdy dress and bonnet, was designed by Sara Lee Creech, sculpted by Sheila Burlingame, and endorsed by Eleanor Roosevelt. It is currently available from Ashton-Drake Galleries.

Say When!: This is a family game by Winning Moves for two players or two teams. All the answers to questions are numbers (some are years in response to the game's name) which players write down on dry-erase boards.

Scattergories: In this game unveiled in 1990 and currently available from Hasbro, two to six players ages twelve and up roll a twenty-sided die with different letters on it and provide words beginning with a selected letter in 144 categories. They must do this before a buzzer sounds at the end of three minutes. At that time, he or she compares answers with the other players. Duplications do not score points, and the player with the most points wins. The set comes with four answer pads, twelve category list cards, a die, a timer, and four pencils. *See* SCRABBLE.

scooters: Actually the earliest form of velocipede, in the form of the hobbyhorse, scooters are an early-twentieth-century toy that witnessed a revival at the end of that century. The simple construction of the scooter consists of a low board that can accommodate both feet, with a wheel in front and back, and a steering column with a bar at the top. The foldable, silver-colored, friction-braked Razor brand scooter of the late 1990s appealed to baby-boomer adults as well as to children. Other contemporary brands include Atomic Cyclone Rush Rider and the Huffy Micro Folding Aluminum. Many have handbars that adjust to different heights, friction brakes in the rear fender, foam grips, and wheels available in different colors. There are also versions with motors and senior-friendly varieties with seats.

Scrabble: This classic crossword game played with Vermont maple wooden tiles was originally invented by out-of-work architect Alfred Mosher Butts from Poughkeepsie, New York. First marketed in 1948 as Lexico, Butts renamed it Criss-Cross Words. Studying the front page of *The New York Times,* Butts estimated how often letters were used in English. James Brunot, Butts's business partner, decided to include only four tiles with the letter S, hoping to limit plurals. In 1948 it was renamed Scrabble (meaning to grope frantically); it was "discovered" by a Macy's executive and licensed to Selchow & Righter in 1952. That company purchased the trademark to Scrabble in 1972, Coleco purchased Selchow & Righter in 1986, and Hasbro purchased Coleco in 1989. In the United States and Canada, Hasbro, Inc. currently owns the trademark; elsewhere, Mattel, Inc. does. In

1996, Hasbro introduced the Scrabble CD-ROM. Since imitation is a very sincere form of flattery, Scrabble's popularity led to versions introduced by competing companies. In 1953, Parker Brothers debuted Keyword while Cadaco in 1954 produced Skip-A-Cross. J. Pressman's game Wordy is almost identical to Scrabble (and may have been based on Criss-Cross Words) except that the letter tiles are color-coded, with each color keyed to a particular point value.

Scrabble is for players ages eight and up (and for two to four players). People build crosswords for points and add to their scores by building words on special spaces on the game board. Players can use up all seven of their letter tiles on their turns for an extra fifty points. Most Scrabble champions are computer scientists or engineers. Words are merely weapons, but strategy is the name of the game.

Specialty versions of Scrabble consist of a golf edition with a golf-term list and a Scrabble Junior Curious George version for ages five and up. This latter for two to four players has twenty-eight yellow hats as scoring chips.

Scruples: This game, introduced in 1986 by Milton Bradley and still obtainable from Hasbro, poses moral dilemmas to three or more adult players related to work, money, family, friends, and relationships. Containing 252 dilemma cards, thirty-six reply cards (reading yes, no, or depends), and twelve ballot cards, players win points by guessing how their opponents may answer. They vote on how their colleagues will act by either holding up a ballot card marked with a halo indicating sincerity or one decorated with a pitchfork indicating a bluff. Players get five yellow dilemma cards, one red reply card, and ballot cards. The first player to dispose of all his or her dilemma cards wins. *See* THE DR. LAURA GAME.

Sea-Monkeys: Marketed as the "original" instant life since 1960 and guaranteed to live for two years, Sea-Monkeys are small crustaceous plankton in suspended animation that are reinvigorated when added to water. Still promoted by its discoverer Harold von Braunhut from Transcience of Bryans Road, Maryland, this "toy" is similar to ant farms in its aim to instruct the purchaser about science.

Shape by Shape: This variation of the ancient Chinese game of tangrams is for ages eight and up by Binary Arts. It consists of fourteen puzzle pieces that fit into a 8-by-5 ¼-inch frame. Players try to match the pieces to sixty different images on challenge cards (which contain hints to solutions on the back). The game offers diversion for participants at many levels of expertise.

Shenanigans: To advertise its own line of games, Milton Bradley in 1964 created a children's Saturday morning program (which also appeared in a home version). Stubby Kaye hosted the television show which featured a series of boardwalk-style games of chance. This children's game bore some similarities to Milton Bradley's Video Village game of 1960. This was based on a television game show (airing from 1960-1962) also played like a board game. Players on the program served as their own game pieces moving across the board.

Silly Putty: Silly Putty was the invention of James Wright, a chemical engineer in New Haven's General Electric plant, or perhaps of Dr. Earl Warrick, as a synthetic substitute for rubber during World War II. This boric acid and silicone oil combination had strange properties. It was not practical as a rubber replacement but it bounced higher than rubber, stretched, and was able to lift images off newspapers. After a stint as a cocktail party curiosity, Ruth Fallgatter (a toy store owner) and Peter Hodgson (a marketing consultant) marketed it as Bouncing Putty, a novelty gift for adults.

In 1950, Hodgson signed Doubleday bookstores at the New York Toy Fair to market the compound. An item in *The New Yorker* popularized the product in the egg-shaped container. In 1990, fluorescent colors were added to the traditional peach color. Despite its lack of claims to practicality, people have used Silly Putty as ear plugs, to clean typewriters' keys, and to remove lint from clothing. This "solid liquid" has with time had more difficulty lifting comics off newspapers that use newer printing techniques. But it remains a best-seller, especially since it appeals to both boys and girls (and was marketed that way from the beginning).

The Simpsons: The United States' longest-running animated series (set to become the situation comedy with the greatest longevity of all time) first aired on the FOX network in 1989. Replete with cultural references, risqué situations, and postmodern family values, this cartoon primarily for adult viewers has resulted in a surfeit of dolls and other toys. *The Simpsons*—Loser Takes All is Roseart's board game for two to six players ages eight and up who compete to win by losing the most of the character cards they are dealt. The game features junk food tokens, not a lot of fake money, and 400 questions on twenty loser cards. In 2002 Hasbro's Milton Bradley line hawked *The Simpsons* Rubik's Cube. This takeoff on the classic 1980s puzzle, for players eight and above, is in the shape of Homer Simpson's head.

slingshots: A war toy that can be used as a real weapon (and was so utilized at least as far back as the days of David and Goliath), slingshots were commercialized and marketed in the mid-twentieth century. Like pick-up-sticks, slingshots were another easily homemade toy that manufacturers turned out quite readily. These "wrist rockets" could be quite dangerous. A slingshot iconically and warily hung out of the back pocket of the character Dennis the Menace. Partners Dick Knerr and Spud Melin designed a slingshot to toss meatballs for falcons and then formed a company with the onomatopoeic sound of hitting a target—Wham-O—to market the design. Howard Ellenburg also improved the slingshot, this time with a metal brace, and founded the company Trumark (which also indicated the purpose of his product).

Slinky: This toy originated as a meter for testing horsepower on battleships. A torsion spring fell off marine engineer Richard James's desk and he was inspired. James took it home to his wife Betty and he refashioned it to allow the spring to walk down stairs. Betty found a dictionary word to describe the toy as "stealthy, sleek, and sinuous." They definitely seemed to have a lifelike quality. In 1945, James demonstrated the Slinky during the Christmas season at Gimbel's Department Store and within ninety minutes sold all 400 that he had. Slinky can serve as a toy, a stress reliever, a demonstration of physics principles, an exercise device, a gutter protector, and a makeshift radio antenna. A standard Slinky contains eighty feet of wire that is now coated for durability and crimped for safety. Variations of Slinky include pull toys with Slinkies as bodies, such as the dachshund in the movie *Toy Story* and caterpillars and trains. Originally coppery in color, later Slinkies were silver in appearance.

Slinky was first immortalized in 1962 in a famous television jingle:

> What walks the stairs, without a care / and shoots so high in the sky? Bounces up and down, just like a clown? / Everyone knows

it's Slinky — / the best present yet to give as a gift, but costs so little to buy. / The hit of the day when you're ready to play — / everyone knows it's Slinky. / It's Slinky, it's Slinky, for fun it's a wonderful toy, / it's Slinky, it's Slinky, the favorite of girls and boys. / Everyone wants a Slinky, / you ought to get a Slinky.

Soakies: Colgate-Palmolive's character plastic bubble-bath bottles first appeared in the 1960s as Disney figures as well as Mighty Mouse, Rocky and Bullwinkle, and Alvin and the Chipmunks. Later Soaky figures include Warner Brothers and *Sesame Street* characters. The 1960s television jingle went: "Soaky soaks you clean in oceans full of fun, / scruppedy bubbledly, flippedty flupedly, clean before you're done. / Soaky soaks you clean and every girl and boy / gets a toy when it's empty, when it's empty it's a toy." The boy in the ad concluded: "Taking a Soaky bath is fun—more fun than getting dirty."

Spare-Time Bowling: A game originating in the 1940s and currently available from ThinkFun, Spare-Time Bowling is for two or more players ages eight and up. It uses special dice with symbols instead of numbers for strikes, spares, splits, and other arrangements of pins knocked down. The set contains a score pad, pencil, ten dice, a plastic bowling pin cup used to roll and store the dice, and instructions.

Spirograph: The invention of the English mechanical engineer Dennis Fischer, this art toy was introduced at the Nuremburg Toy Fair in 1965. Kenner acquired the rights to it. This unique toy has gears to make concentric patterns and is meant for children five to seven years old. The set includes seven plastic gears, one gear template, one drawing template, paper, and an idea book. This toy is often used in the classroom. Its emphasis on visual-motor skills makes it especially useful for the instruction of children with physical and learning disabilities.

spy toys: The 1960s saw a profusion of motion pictures and television programs about spies. In 1965, A. C. Gilbert was licensed to produce a twelve-inch action figure of Sean Connery's James Bond, Agent 007, and his nemesis Oddjob. Gilbert also issued smaller plastic figures of Bond, Miss Moneypenny, Dr. No, Goldfinger, and Oddjob. In 1978, Mego introduced Roger Moore's version of Bond and other characters from *Moonraker* in twelve-inch versions. Gilbert also created 1965's television spy characters Napoleon Solo and Iilya Kuryakin from *The Man from U.N.C.L.E.* In 1967, Marx introduced the doll April Dancer from *The Girl from U.N.C.L.E.* In the 1990s, McFarlane Toys introduced action figures from the movie *Austin Powers.*

Square Root Puzzle: In this eponymous toy from the Square Root company, the player is challenged to maneuver the largest of ten wooden squares through a slot at the bottom of a frame without removing or touching any of the other pieces. It usually takes over eighty moves to accomplish this, so persistence is rewarded. This game is still on the market.

Stormy Seas: Binary Arts currently offers this maritime version of Rush Hour for ages eight and up. This is a navigation game in which skippers try to find an open channel to steer their boats to a safe harbor. It contains forty cards and features four ascending levels of difficulty. As with several other products of this company, this contains a storage tray for the playing pieces. *See* RUSH HOUR.

Stratego: Since 1961, Stratego has been Milton Bradley's classic game of battlefield strategy for ages eight and up. Players call upon memory, planning, and luck to find and capture an enemy's flags before their own are discovered. In the classic board version, each player starts with an army of men and six bombs. The game is also available in computerized versions.

strategy board games: Chess, checkers, backgammon, and Go are among examples of games in which the contestant with the better strategy triumphs. A great many board games rely on strategy while others are more dependent on luck and the roll of the dice, as in Monopoly.

Strawberry Shortcake: In 1979, American Greetings debuted this character in a series of cards. Due to its popularity, Kenner introduced a scented line of dolls in the early 1980s. Soon there was a television show (in effect, one long commercial) built specifically around these toys. Like the confection after which they were named, these programs were known for their sweetness. With 1980s nostalgia these dolls came back into favor after the turn of the millennium.

The *Survivor* Game: Mattel's game for four to eight adult players based on the popular CBS television program debuted in the fall 2000 season. The game dares participants to meet challenges, vote, and strategize. As on the show, there is an immunity idol and teams merge.

Susie Smart: A large child-sized doll sold in supermarkets that came in a school-desk and had a blackboard, Susie Smart could recite and count. This primary school pupil was quite a contrast to the reviled 1992 version of Teen Talk Barbie who complained that "math class is tough." But perhaps they did realistically reflect their different eras.

Suzy Cute: This was Topper Toys' 1960s doll advertised in song by the inimitable Louis Armstrong. When a girl pressed Suzy's stomach, her arms went up. The ad concluded, "Suzy Cute needs a mommy . . . Suzy Cute needs you."

Sweet Sue Sophisticates (1957): These pre-Barbie offerings were American Character's fourteen-, twenty-, and twenty-five-inch fashion dolls with high-heeled feet. Sweet Sue had jointed ankles for wearing either flat shoes or high-heels.

T

talking dolls: Although several versions appeared in the early 1960s, in 1889 Thomas Edison actually patented and produced a sophisticated working phonograph doll. This had a perforated metal body (which emitted nursery rhymes) and a bisque head, but many others were to appear in the interactive, loquacious 1960s. *See* CHATTY CATHY; SUSIE SMART.

Tamagotchi: "Virtual pets" introduced by Bandai Co. in the 1990s, these are cyber creatures depicted on a small digital screen on a colorful, round, plastic electronic device. The caregiver administers to his or her pet with a series of buttons. Lack of regular attention results in a mean-spirited and later, a departed, pet. The Giga Pets version comes as a key chain. *See* FURBIES.

Tammy: Ideal's wholesome teenage fashion doll, introduced in 1962, was popular with girls and their parents. Ideal licensed her name to other toy companies which produced accompanying dishes, housewares, and other items. Tammy had many friends, among them Pepper, Pos'n Pete, Pos'n Salty, Dodi, and Ted.

teddy bears: The teddy bear, named after Theodore Roosevelt, debuted with the partly mythical story of how the president spared the life of a wounded cub on November 14, 1902, while on a hunting trip in the South. *The Washington Post*'s political cartoonist Clifford Berryman popularized this report in his *Drawing the Line in Mississippi.* The president was visiting there because of a boundary dispute between that state and Louisiana. Although in actuality, Roosevelt put the wounded bear out of its misery by shooting it while it was tethered rather than releasing it and hunting it down, the fable of the fuzzy character escaping from a hunted death endeared itself to Berryman's readers.

Adolph Gund established his soft toy company in Norwalk, Connecticut, in 1898. Around 1900 the company moved to Manhattan, its manufacturing and sales center. Gund began manufacturing teddy bears to take advantage of the story and is currently the leading U.S. manufacturer of them. In 1922 Gund secured the license for Crazy Kat, which later evolved into Felix the Cat. In 1925, Gund sold his company to Jacob Swedlin. Gund, Inc. moved to Brooklyn in 1957 and to Edison, New Jersey, in 1971. Noted for quality plush toys, Gund's stuffing has changed over the years from excelsior or wood shavings, to kapok, cotton, and then to rubber or silicone fiber.

Another account has Morris Michtom, who owned a cigar and candy store in Brooklyn, producing a prototype of a plush bear and displaying it in his store window as "Teddy's Bear." After a note sent to the president asking for permission to market it under Roosevelt's name received a positive response, Michtom got into the business under the Ideal company, which he founded.

The German firm Steiff (which marked its bears with a signature button in their ears, "Klopf Im Ohr," as well as a seam down their felt faces) is another early famous manufacturer of teddy bears. Kenner's 1983 twist on this was the Care Bears line of books and products. Care Bears is a line of twelve plush figures each marked with a symbol on its stomach indicating a different positive emotion. All the bears have plastic hearts hidden within their fur on their backsides. Originally created as a character for cards by American Greetings in 1981, Kenner's multiplicity of figures encouraged children (and their parents) to buy more than one. Among the nurtured emotions were love, friendship, trust, and good sportsmanship. There were six television specials in 1985 and cinematic releases, *The Care Bears Movie* (1985) and *The Care Bears Movie II: A New Generation* (1986).

A hit of 1985 was Teddy Ruxpin. Worlds of Wonder was undoubtedly inspired by Disneyland's animatronic animals and supplied this teddy with his own audiotaped voice. Knickerbocker Teddy Bears offered a Winston the Fertility Bear which is supposed to foster human conception (but doesn't really, of course). This followed in the tradition of the impact of the teddy bear on popular culture. Today there are VIP Teddy Bears in the guise of Abraham Lincoln, Charlie Chaplin, and Mr. Spock of Star Trek. Naples, Florida, features a Teddy Bear Museum.

The British version of the teddy bear is Winnie-the-Pooh, which has lent its immense popularity to puzzles and board games as well as to plush playthings. The Pooh Bear originated in children's poems published in the 1920s by English writer A. A. Milne. The bear and his human companion Christopher Robin soon thereafter appeared in storybooks. More recently Winnie-the-Pooh has appeared in a series of animated Disney films starting with *Winnie the Pooh and the Honey Tree* in 1966. The late actor Sterling Holloway provided the voice for the British bear.

Teletubbies: Hasbro's Playskool line came out with a toy version of the late 1990s British export to American PBS television that is safe for all ages. Seeking a niche for the incipient preschool televiewer (and receiving their share of criticism for attempting to snag this group), the Teletubby characters predictably emitted monosyllabic sounds. The four characters were brightly colored, including the most talked about, Tinky Winky. In bright violet attire and purportedly carrying a handbag, he aroused controversy as a possible gay icon.

television quiz shows: Many games first appearing as television quiz shows issued home versions, often at first as premiums or consolation prizes for their own contestants. These board games later were sold in stores. Among these shows were *Concentration* (based on guessing parts of rebuses); *Jeopardy* (supplying the correct questions to answers, rising in difficulty according to how much they were worth);

Password (a word association game); and *Say When* (the contestant closest to the correct answer expressed in the form of a number scores). Other popular games included *The Price Is Right* (Lowell, 1958); *Beat the Clock* (Lowell, 1955); Groucho Marx's *You Bet Your Life* (Lowell, 1955); and *Play Your Hunch* (Transogram, 1960).

Three-dimensional board games were prominent in the early 1960s. The Ideal Toy Company introduced Mouse Trap and Kaboom while Transogram produced Green Ghost in 1965, a glow-in-the-dark game. Its game Kabala in 1967 was an unsuccessful blend of Green Ghost and the traditional Ouija board. Other surreal games of the intense Cold War era of the early 1960s included: Haunted House (Ideal, 1962); King Zor (Ideal, 1963—based on *St. George and the Dragon*); King Kong (Ideal, 1963); Godzilla (Ideal, 1963); Weird Oh's (Ideal, 1964); Outer Limits (Milton Bradley, 1964); The Twilight Zone (Ideal, 1964—not as inspired as its namesake television program); Mystic Skull (Ideal, 1964); Kreskin's ESP (Milton Bradley, 1967); and Voodoo Doll Game (Schaper, 1967). *See others under their respective names.*

Think-a-Tron: An electronic game imitating early computers that used punch cards, Hasbro's Think-a-Tron from the early 1960s was marketed as "The Machine That Thinks Like a Man!" The plastic component unit came in aqua blue accented with gray and white, with a black background behind clear bulbs that lit up when the machine was activated. Three hundred questions translated into patterns on punch cards were fed into the machine. The answers that came out were authenticated by *The Book of Knowledge, The Children's Encyclopedia.* See ELECTRONIC GAMES.

Tickle Me Elmo: This is Mattel's late-1990s plush version of the *Sesame Street* PBS television program character, the invention of the late puppeteer Jim Henson. Elmo's battery-operated device let out peals of laughter, which predictably delighted children and often irked adults.

Tiddlywinks: A British game in origin that has many adherents among Anglophiles in the United States, tiddlywinks is basically a game of strategy, tactics, manual dexterity, and intellectual activity whereby players flick plastic counters into a cup. The name derives from "tiddlywink," English slang for an unlicensed pub, and the game was quintessentially a pub activity. Four players arranged in two pairs (in singles matches, each player takes care of two sets of colored counters) capture enemy counters (winks) by covering them up with counters of their own. Each set has six pieces, four winks, and two squidgers. Blue always partners red and green partners yellow. Starting off in the four corners of a mat, players use large counters called squidgers to flick smaller winks into a central cup. Players can have different squidgers for different kinds of shots. Winks often are stacked on top of each other to form piles during the game. Its aficionados liken it to three-dimensional chess.

The goal is to secure the highest number of table points (tiddlies). Three tiddlies are scored for each wink in the pot and one for each wink that remains uncovered by other winks. The player scoring the most tiddlies gets four game points, the player who comes in second gets two points, and the player coming in third garners one point. Partners add their points together. There are always seven points in every game.

If one player gets all of his or her six winks into the pot he or she wins by potting out. Any winks covered are then released and two more colors must also put their winks into the pot to distribute the seven points. It is rare for the game to end with all of the winks in the pot. Competition is often intense as evidenced by such slang expressions as to bomb—to project a wink at a pile in the hope of disturbing it—and "good shot." Named after John Good, this is the playing of a wink through a nearby pile in the hope of destroying it.

The game dates back to the end of the nineteenth century. Joseph Fincher filed for the first patent in 1888. Enthusiasm for the modern game began among undergraduates at Christ's College, Cambridge, in 1955. Oxford entered the collegiate fray within three years. Oxford players took the game to the United States in 1961 under the sponsorship of Guiness. It established itself at the Massachusetts Institute of Technology whose teams frequently competed in Britain. Some modern, sports-themed versions have pieces resembling miniature tennis rackets, horseshoes, and the like. *See* POGS.

Time Bomb: Milton Bradley's 1964 version of hot potato, this black plastic globe can be wound up and tossed from player to player. Anyone holding it when it goes off is eliminated, as is the person to whom it is tossed when it is in midair.

Tinkertoys: This was the invention of stonemason Charles Pajeau of Evanston, Illinois, in 1913 who was inspired by the ingenuity of his own children at play. He had observed them sticking pencils into empty spools of thread and then building things with them. Pajeau created a shorter, wheellike spool with a hole in the center and several along the sides. He and his business partner, stockbroker Robert Petit, called themselves the Toy Tinkers and marketed the "Thousand Wonder Builder." Selling directly to Chicago-area pharmacies and stores, these entrepreneurs set up elaborate displays of completed projects. When they did the same at New York's Grand Central Station, the toy's sales took off.

Changes have taken place over the years. The unpainted wood was gradually replaced, first by red sticks in 1953, then with the addition of green, yellow, and blue sticks in 1955. Since 1992, the spools and sticks are not only bigger and longer but made entirely of plastic. Recent retro revivals have resulted in the familiar wooden sets once gain packaged in cardboard cylinders with metal ends. Another competing version of Tinkertoys is Fiddlestix. A. C. Gilbert considered Tinkertoys to be the principal rival to his erector sets. Tinkertoys' versatility, stability, and relative ease of construction actually made them more accessible to more children than were erector sets. Many scientific and architectural museums give a place to Tinkertoys, often alongside Erector Sets and Lincoln Logs. Since the 1980s Tinkertoys have been marketed by Hasbro. *See* ERECTOR SET; LINCOLN LOGS.

Tiny Tears: A doll of the 1960s by American Character, Tiny Tears had rock-a-bye eyes that slowly closed when moved from side to side. She also "cried" after being fed water from a bottle (in a variation of what Betsy Wetsy did), wet, and blew bubbles when squeezed.

Tiny Thumbelina: An early 1960s soft vinyl doll made by the Ideal Company, Thumbelina is fifteen inches long with a plastic windup knob on her back that makes her wriggle just like a real baby.

Toni doll (1949-1954): This commercial tie-in made by Ideal allowed its owners to give home permanent waves to the Toni doll (offered by the Toni Company). Presumably, with this doll they would be more inclined to sit still while getting their own hair curled.

Tootsietoy: American manufacturer Charles Dowst found inspiration at the 1893 Chicago Columbian Exposition when he observed a Linotype machine produce small metal objects from liquid metal put into a model. In 1906, he began making small toy cars this way. In 1922, Dowst Manufacturing made dollhouse furniture using the die-cast method and named them Tootsietoy after the nickname of his granddaughter. In 1924, his company took this name. Among non–die-cast products for which Tootsietoy was famous was bubble solution. But Tootsietoy was most renowned for toy die-cast cars. In the 1960s, Tootsietoy merged with Strombecker, a specialist in plastic toys. Since 1969, when the last all-metal toy car was cast, Tootsietoy has included plastic parts.

tops: Spinning tops have been among the oldest of toys, perhaps originating in Asia thousands of years ago. Around the Jewish festival of Hanukkah, four-sided tops marked with Hebrew letters, called dreidels, are spun in a game of chance. Wooden whip tops were placed into motion through the quick release of strings wound around them. The yo-yo operates on a similar principle and hence was sometimes called a "return top." In the early twentieth century, lithographed tin tops were popular. Sometimes emitting music while spinning, and often decorated with rainbow colors or circus motifs, these tops were pumped by a wooden grip handle. As a sign of their continuing vibrancy, University Games in 1998 began merchandising Doodle-top—The Top That Actually Draws for those ages five and up. The Doodletop activity kit comes equipped with short felt-tipped pens of various colors on five tops, paper, and a booklet showing how to play games of skill with these spinning devices. The artistic results often look like Spirograph products.

toy soldiers: Originally composed of iron, then of lead, and finally of plastic, toy soldiers often had rounded flat discs attached to their feet to allow them to stand upright. They were frequently sold in bulk (no doubt reflecting the vast numbers produced by conscript armies) and were the targets of children's slingshots and BB guns. The advent of

G.I. Joe and other named action figures diminished the popularity of these soldiers beginning in the 1960s.

toys in movies: Movie references to childhood objects are numerous, including the famous sled Rosebud in *Citizen Kane* (1941) and the Red Ryder BB gun in *A Christmas Story* (1983). Tom Hanks ran wild in New York's FAO Schwarz toy store in *Big* (1988). The two versions of *Toy Story,* however, featured these main playthings as active agents, with the human beings around them as supporting actors. In *Toy Story* (1995), the first full-length computer-animated film, a little boy's world is upset by the arrival of Buzz Lightyear (voice of Tim Allen), a space ranger, who usurps the favored place of Woody (Tom Hanks), the cowboy plaything. Buzz must address the discomforting fact that he is not a real astronaut. The toys are forced to work together (thereby supplying the film's moral) in order to get home after they are lost. Don Rickles (Mr. Potato Head), Jim Varney (Slinky Dog), John Ratzenberger (Hamm, the piggy bank), Annie Potts, and Laurie Metcalf supplied other voices.

In *Toy Story 2* (1999), the boy Andy goes off to summer camp, leaving behind his toys. This allows the evil collector Al McWhiggin (Wayne Knight) to kidnap Woody and attempt to sell him to a Japanese toy museum. There are moral confrontations when the Howdy-Doody-like Woody must decide whether he would prefer to be reunited with his owner (and with the toy companions who seek to rescue him) or lead a sterile but presumably eternal life behind glass with other classic toys. The sophisticated humor and cultural references made these films appeal to adults as well as children.

trains: First introduced at the 1893 Columbian Exposition in Chicago, electric trains had their most popular American incarnations in the lines produced by Lionel and American Flyer. New York–based Joshua Lionel Cowen first decorated Ingersoll's Department Store window with his Electric Express in 1901. Personal orders soon led to manufacture for home use of trains powered by either dry cell batteries or electric current. In 1934 Lionel exhibited the "Train of Tomorrow" at the Chicago Century of Progress Exposition. Also in that year, the company unveiled the Mickey Mouse Handcar, featuring the popular rodent and his companion Minnie.

A. C. Gilbert took over the Chicago-based American Flyer line in 1938. Although electric trains experienced their golden age in the 1920s (and a recent thirty-two-cent U.S. postage stamp celebrating that decade recognizes this), they survived the Great Depression and revived after World War II as a pastime geared to fathers and sons. Lionel's annual illustrated catalogs became almost as collectable as the trains that they featured.

Although the major toy train makers did produce landscaping features (and Lionel in particular made working coal elevators, water towers, etc.), some other companies specialized in this feature. One notable example is Bachmann Brothers, a Philadelphia firm. In 1946, they began a Plasticville U.S.A. line of vibrantly colored injection-molded plastic buildings, picket fences, figures, automobiles, and trees. Lionel miscalculated its specific appeal to girls, a group that had been neglected in the company's advertising. This resulted in 1957's debut of a pastel set with a pink locomotive, yellow boxcar, light blue caboose, and white and gold transformer. Many girls liked trains but they preferred to play with the realistic ones that their brothers had. This train's sales were dismal but it is now a collector's item. In the 1960s, some Lionel trains had Cold War–style secret launching pads inside sidecars for military reconnaissance missions.

Transformers: In 1984 Hasbro introduced Transformers, ordinary objects such as cars and planes that children could manipulate to change into robot figures. Generation 1 (from 1984-1990) comprised items such as Autobots, which turned into vehicles, as well as Decepticons (with three modes of change), Headmasters (vehicles that turned into weapons), Powermasters, Pretender Beasts, Micromasters, and Action Masters. Insecticons from 1985 turned into make-believe insects. The popularity of these items was spurred by the 1984 *The Transformers* animated television series, Marvel comic books of the same year, and the 1986 *Transformers: The Movie.*

In 1987 Sixshot premiered as the first transformer with six modes of change. The year 1989 saw the Micromasters line of miniature transformers. In 1990, Action Masters appeared as articulated figures based on transformer characters. After no new products surfaced during 1990-1991, Generation 2 surfaced in 1992 and lasted until 1995. Several of these offerings had electric sounds. The years 1996 to 1999 witnessed the Beast Wars line based on a new animated televison series. In 1998 came Fuzors, robots whose beast stages combined two different animals. Transmetals were transformers that developed metal superstructures. As testimony to the pull of nostalgia for collectibles not yet in the distant past, the years 2001-2002 saw the return of the Autobots and Decepticons.

Trivial Pursuit: Trivial Pursuit, advertised as "a party in a box," is an interactive card-based question and answer game invented in Montreal by several friends. It was the result of the happy collaboration of Scott Abbott, Chris Haney, his brother John Haney, and Ed Werner. Trivial Pursuit debuted at the International Toy Fair in New York in February 1982. Because of its high ticket price, both Parker Brothers and Milton Bradley passed on it. Selchow & Righter became its U.S. distributor in 1983, and it became the breakout best-selling adult game of that Christmas season. In 1988, Parker Brothers, then a part of Tonka, acquired the rights to it. In 1992, these rights passed on to Hasbro when that company acquired Parker Brothers.

Originally supposed to be called Trivia Pursuit, Sarah Haney, Chris's wife, suggested otherwise. Each question in Trivial Pursuit must begin with who, where, what, or how? It is designed for two to six players or teams and comes in many specialized versions and editions (over forty-five and counting) with unique questions in each set. Among them are Trivial Pursuit Genus 5; Trivial Pursuit Junior (for players eight and up); Trivial Pursuit Edition 6 (containing 4,800 new queries on people, places, art and entertainment, history, science and nature, and sports and leisure); the Trivial Pursuit Pop Culture DVD Game; specialized subject sets, such as Silver Screen, Young Players, Baby Boomers, and Music editions; a 20th Anniversary Edition released in 2002 (containing 3,600 questions covering events from 1982-2002); and the Trivial Pursuit *Lord of the Rings* Movie Trilogy Collector's Edition. In 2003, Handmark released a handheld version of this enormously popular and transmutable game. *See* MINDTRAP.

troll dolls: Trolls are legendary Scandinavian folktale creatures, reputedly old people, who lived under bridges or in caves. They could be either dwarves or giants. The story "The Three Billy Goats Gruff" features a troll under a bridge. Thomas Dam, a Danish wood-carver, created the first small elfin troll for mass marketing in the 1960s.

These three- to eight-inch-high dolls experienced a revival in the 1980s.

Dam began making trolls for auction out of vinyl and filled with sawdust. Manufacturers other than Dam are the Wishnik variety, made by Uneeda Doll Co.; Treasure Trolls with Wishstones in their tummies by Ace Novelty Co. Inc.; and those by Russ (Russ Bernie and Co. Inc.); and Scandia House. As collectibles, trolls are often called so ugly that they are cute. It is no surprise, therefore, that they first gained popularity in the United States during the "alternative" decades of the 1960s and 1970s.

Trouble: This is a Milton Bradley game for players six to nine years old featuring Popomatic dice (that children cannot eat or lose). The first player to move all four of his or her pegs around the game board and across the finish line wins. You can bump others back—if you get caught, you're in trouble.

Twenty One: In 1956 Lowell produced a board game version of the smash NBC quiz show with the "soundproof" booths that purportedly ensured the honesty of the games. In 1958, the famous quiz show scandals erupted around this program with the disclosure that popular contestants such as Charles Van Doren received the correct answers ahead of time.

25 Words or Less: This game for ages nine and up by Winning Moves, "The Game Where Every Word Counts . . .," requests short answers to queries such as a dog itcher?—flea; innie or outie?—belly button.

Twisted Toys: These parodies of Beanie Baby toys have names like Dopeyman (a yellow creature with a dunce cap); No-Fur-Be, a furless toy; and Teletushy, a purple lush.

Twister: "The Game That Ties You Up in Knots," this Milton Bradley game for children and adults was introduced in 1966. Charles Foley, the inventor, at first presented it with the name Pretzel because the dance the Twist was then in declining popularity. But the name Twister was selected to avoid competing with another toy called Pretzel then being marketed by Ideal.

With each spin of the wheel, a player must move a hand or a foot to a different colored circle on a vinyl mat. As it becomes harder to stay in balance, the first one to fall loses. For two to four players, it encouraged opposite-sex interaction (as Johnny Carson amply demonstrated when he played it with Eva Gabor on *The Tonight Show*) although it is advertised for ages six and up. As with the introduction of rock and roll ten years earlier, some people questioned the morality of this game. But the times had truly changed and Twister has remained a popular icebreaker. The fact that it uses enlarged dots rather than text makes it appealing to all age groups (and to those unfamiliar with English as well).

In 1968 Milton Bradley put out Grab A Loop. The goal of this follow-up to Twister was for players to stay away from each other to protect their colored loops. In 1969 Milton Bradley put Limbo Legs on the market, a game which also promoted group interaction. Its direct spinoff called Animal Twister was on the market for only three years because it cut into the original Twister's sales.

Uncle Wiggily: In 1916 Milton Bradley unveiled this game based on the Uncle Wiggily Bedtime Stories of Howard R. Garis. The elderly rabbit Uncle Wiggily Longears had first appeared as a storybook character in 1910. Milton Bradley kept exclusive control of this children's board game until 1967, when Parker Brothers received the rights to it. In 1989, Bradley reintroduced a necessarily different version with the blessing of Garis's daughter-in-law. Since that time, in the Parker version, the winning player reaches Dr. Possum's office, number 151 on the board. In the Bradley abbreviated variant, there is no Dr. Possum and the winner lands on space 100.

UNO: UNO was invented in 1971 by Merle Robbins, an Ohio barbershop owner. International Games, Inc. first marketed it. In 1992, International Games became part of Mattel, the game's current distributor. UNO contains instructions and 108 cards arranged in the following categories: nineteen blue cards from 0-9; nineteen green cards from 0-9; nineteen red cards from 0-9; nineteen yellow cards from 0-9; eight Draw Turn cards–two each in the four colors; eight Reverse

Cards–two each in the four colors; eight Skip Cards–two each in the four colors; four Wild Cards; and four Wild Draw Four cards.

Players are dealt seven cards with the remaining going to a Draw Pile. The first card on the Draw Pile is turned up to form a Discard Pile. Each player in turn must match the top card on the Discard Pile by number, color, or symbol (such as a Wild Card). If a player cannot make a match, he or she must draw a card from the top of the Draw Pile. The player either matches that card or passes. The winner, disposing of all his or her cards, scores 500 points.

Upwords—The 3-Dimensional Word Game That Really Stacks Up!: A high-powered version of Scrabble designed by Elliott Rudell for Milton Bradley for ages ten and up, in Upwords players can stack letters on top of tiles already on the board to make new words. Scoring is easier—each tile earns two points and each stacked pile earns one point. As in Scrabble, capitalized, abbreviated, and hyphenated words are prohibited. Upwords moves more quickly than Scrabble and is better for those with limited vocabularies. It rewards the player for sharing letters but not for using tougher letters. Upwords is designed for two to four players. *See* SCRABBLE.

View-Master: The invention of William Gruber, a piano tuner from Portland, Oregon, this device permits the viewing of three-dimensional color slides in a compact viewer with two eyepieces. It consists of fourteen small slides on a circular card that create seven images for individual viewing. Gruber teamed up with Harold Graves, president of Sawyer's Photographic Services, to manufacture the first View-Master. View-Master was first marketed in Gruber's hometown and featured nature scenes. It was introduced nationally at the New York and San Francisco World's Fairs of 1939.

From 1942 through 1945, the army and navy ordered special View-Masters for training in ship and aircraft identification. Sawyer's, the camera shop that marketed View-Master, in 1951 purchased Tru-View a rival filmstrip firm. This gave access to licensed Disney characters and launched the product as a successful children's toy. In 1966 GAF (General Aniline and Film Corporation) bought Sawyer. With this purchase came more television and movie tie-ins. Today View-Master also comes in the form of a Super Show (wall and ceiling) Projector and a Virtual Viewer with a wraparound visor to immerse the viewer. But the version closer to the original is more soothing and a rather singular activity.

War toys: *See* CAP GUNS; G. I. JOE; TOY SOLDIERS.

Wheel-O: Invented in Patterson, New Jersey, in 1953, the Wheel-O is a curved piece of wire and a 2.5-inch red plastic wheel with a magnet in its core. This allows the wheel to roll without falling off.

whirligigs: Folk-art type of primitive figures made of wood that turn when the wind hits its paddles. These may be in the form of arms or wings. *See* PINWHEELS.

Who Wants to Be a Millionaire: This is a home version by Pressman of the smash television show of 1999 originally hosted by Regis Philbin that many competitors tried, but failed, to imitate. This game asks fifteen questions (out of a total of almost 2,000) of increasing difficulty and offers the player a limited number of "lifelines" for assistance. He or she can phone a friend at home or poll the "audience" (who are fellow players, that is, competitors). Not to be confused with Hasbro's You Just Became a Millionaire, which challenges players to plan what to do with a windfall.

Why: This was a Milton Bradley game introduced in 1958 as a tie-in to *Alfred Hitchcock Presents,* the popular television program. Players could take the role of either of four detectives—Dick Crazy, Charlie Clam, Sergeant Monday, and Shylock Bones—trying to locate six different ghosts haunting a house.

Wiffle ball: This was the 1953 invention of former semipro baseball player (turned erstwhile car polish manufacturer) David Mullany. The Wiffle ball permits safe play in constricted suburban areas. After various attempts, Mullany discovered that eight oblong holes at one end allowed the thrown ball to curve.

Named after the 1950s' slang "whiff" for to strike out, the company almost never advertises. The one exception was a television commercial done in 1960 with New York Yankees pitcher Whitey Ford.

windup toys: Windup toys, toys of motion rather than still playthings, were originally composed of tinplate. They portray people, animals, and objects such as vehicles and are powered by springs or clockwork mechanisms. With the latter method of activation, the toy can operate for up to thirty minutes rather than for only two to three minutes using a coil or spring. They first appeared in large quantities in the mid-nineteenth century. Germany was the leading source for such toys until World War I gave American entrepreneurs such as Julius' Chein and company an advantage in their own country when trade was disrupted. U.S. manufacturers, however, had been involved in their production since the nineteenth century. Among Chein's popular products were walkers such as ducks, clowns, and rabbits and carnival toys, among them roller coasters, Ferris wheels, and carousels.

Louis Marx was a prominent manufacturer of windups in the 1930s and 1940s. Among his company's more popular offerings were the Merrymakers Band featuring a group of mouse musicians; the Donald Duck Duet; Popeye the Champ; and L'il Abner and Dogpatch Band. After World War II, low labor costs made occupied Japan a center in the production of windups. With the influx of inexpensive East Asian toys came increasingly more plastic windups. Marx and Lakeside made many of these. Battery-powered toys eventually eclipsed the popularity of windups except among collectors.

Winky Dink: This was a mail-order toy of the mid-1950s (a premium version was available in stores) linked to a popular CBS children's television program *Winky Dink and You.* The basic kit consisted of a green-tinted "magic screen," crayons, and an erasing cloth. The plastic screen allowed kids to draw on the family television set with impunity. The deluxe kit contained a puzzle, more crayons, and a game book. Both mail-order and deluxe varieties were manufactured by Standard Toykraft Products of Brooklyn, New York.

With this early experiment in interactive television, children were invited to draw the protagonist out of difficulties. The attempt at reviving *Winky Dink and You* in 1969 was unsuccessful as parents then did not want their children pressed right against the TV screen.

The Wizard of Oz: Pressman makes two versions of board games based on the perennially popular 1939 Judy Garland movie (now licensed through Turner Entertainment) based on the original 1900 novel by L. Frank Baum. *The Wizard of Oz* Yellow Brick Road Game for two to four players ages three to six does not require contestants to read as they attempt to collect a diploma, a pocket-watch heart, a medal for courage, or ruby slippers. *The Wizard of Oz* Trivia Game for two to four players from ages six to adult has fifty color pictures from the film as well as 1,250 questions for two levels of play, a game board, and rainbow movers.

wooden toys: Wood was the preferred material for toys (and for many other household objects) before metal and later plastic replaced it. It is still mostly used in blocks and Scrabble tiles. In 1903 German immigrant Albert Schoenhut of Philadelphia introduced the Humpty Dumpty circus which had six- to eight-inch jointed wooden animals and performers. In 1911 he introduced jointed "All-Wood Perfection Art Dolls." These had solid wooden heads and hollow bodies with springs that allowed them to hold poses. The company went bankrupt in 1935 because of its largely expensive, high-quality toys.

Wooly Willy: Consisting of iron dust under a clear plastic container over a comical face, this toy allows one to move hair to an initially bald-headed and clean-shaven man. Invented by Donald Herzog in 1951 for the Smethport Specialty Co., he at first marketed it to G. C. Murphy's five-and-dime chain. The original was followed by Dapper

Dan and Brunette Betty as well as Hair-Do Harriet and Whiskers the Cat.

Y

Yahtzee: This is a Milton Bradley game of skill and cunning for players ages eight and up introduced in 1956. Players shake five dice for classic combinations such as full houses, large straights, and five of a kind. The first player with a full scorecard wins. The name derives from the fact that it was first played on a yacht docked in Bermuda. A wealthy couple asked the E.S. Lowe Co. to receive 1,000 sets to give away as gifts in return for the rights to the game. They got their wish.

yo-yos: One of the oldest toys in the world, found in ancient Egyptian tombs, Greece, and China and second only to the doll in longevity, a yo-yo consists of twin discs propelled by a string. In France, at the end of the eighteenth century, this toy was known as "l'emigrette," after the French nobles who enjoyed it (but who left during the revolution). Around 1880, in Great Britain it bore the names bandalore, quiz, *incroyable* (a French term for a dandy), or the Prince of Wales. In 1866, a U.S. patent for an improved bandalore was made but the toy did not make much of an impact until the 1920s.

The Filipino immigrant Pedro Flores, working as a busboy in Santa Monica, California, made a yo-yo in 1928, which he used to amuse guests. Flores introduced it with the Tagalog name, "yo-yo," which means "come back." People in the Philippines had used a variant of it as a weapon and a hunting tool for approximately 400 years before its American debut. The string made it easier to retrieve safely.

Donald F. Duncan, the inventor of the Eskimo Pie frozen confection and the originator of the Good Humor ice cream truck, bought the rights from Flores and began making yo-yos in 1929. Duncan improved some of the toy's technology such as introducing a slip string to substitute for a knot around the axle. This led to particular tricks, such as allowing the yo-yo to "sleep" or rest when spun out with a certain type of motion.

During the 1930s, Duncan's hometown assembly center of Luck, Wisconsin, billed itself as the "yo-yo capital of the world." Hard maple in the area was used for the product. Duncan worked out a deal with William Randolph Hearst for free advertising if competitors in yo-yo contests brought in three new newspaper customers as their entrance fees. This entrepreneur also hired teams of young men wearing white cardigan sweaters to demonstrate yo-yos in stores and school-yards. In time there was a full repertoire of yo-yo tricks.

Duncan trademarked the term yo-yo in 1932 and competitors had to market their products as Royal Return Tops, Whirl a Gigs, or Cheerios. Julius Cayo of Benton Harbor, Michigan, during this decade sold the Musical Ka-Yo, a hollow return top with holes in the rim which whistled when it was spun. Duncan later commissioned Cayo to make tin whistling yo-yos for his company. Some of these were brightly lithographed like Cayo's own models.

Duncan's rainbow versions issued during the 1930s are hot collectibles. Duncan later astutely tapped into the space race phenomenon with the Satellite YoYo in 1960 and the Shrieking Sonic Satellite YoYo Return Top in 1962.

Sales and popularity reached a peak in 1962, although the comedian Tommy Smothers later helped revive yo-yo play. President Richard Nixon opened the Grand Ole Opry in 1974 by playing with a yo-yo. Autographed, it was later sold at auction for thousands of dollars. Duncan filed for bankruptcy in 1965 (which had been brought on by legal expenses and high advertising costs). The Flambeau Plastic Co., which had been making plastic yo-yos for Duncan, soon thereafter bought the name Duncan and its trademarks. All-plastic yo-yos replaced Duncan's wooden (usually maple and sometimes ash and beech) models. The first plastic yo-yos appeared in the 1950s. In 1954, Duncan's Pony Boy Yo-Yo had a BB inside that rattled during play.

There is a national Yo-Yo Museum in Chico, California, and an International Yo-Yo Museum in Tucson, Arizona. The Arizona city now claims the title of yo-yo capital of the world. *See* TOPS.

Toy Inventors, Manufacturers, and Distributors

Amerman, John W. (1932-   ): As Mattel's chairman and CEO, Amerman focused on core products, cutting costs, strategic acquisitions, and reorganizing management.

Armatys, Walter W.: An executive director of Toy Manufacturers of America (TMA), Armatys has managed the annual Toy Fair in New York City for many years. Retired, he served as secretary of the International Committee of Toy Industries.

Bradley, Milton (1836-1911): An early lithographer (whose portrait of Lincoln without his beard was soon outdated), Bradley became an inventor and purveyor of games. He first offered The Checkered Game of Life in 1860. He issued travel games for soldiers during the Civil War. Involved in the kindergarten movement, Bradley wrote on this topic and marketed school items. In 1876, at the Philadelphia Centennial Exposition, his company received an award for the ethical teaching of children through play. His diversions often taught youngsters colors and geographical or historical facts. They instructed adults in moral lessons in contrast to the nondidactic aspects of Parker Brothers' games.

The company which Milton Bradley left behind went through a series of transformations. James Shea rescued it from bankruptcy during the Great Depression and gave it new life. In 1962 it broke ground at East Longmeadow, Massachusetts, looking toward an expansion. Finally, in 1984 Milton Bradley and its subsidiary, Playskool, Inc. (for infants, toddlers, and primary school children) were acquired by Hasbro. But the name Milton Bradley carries so much market (and nostalgic) value that Hasbro continues to sell products under that name. *See* SHEA, JAMES J.

Breslow, Jeffrey; Morrison, Howard; and Terzian, Reuben: This triumvirate formed a toy creation and design team from 1967 to 1998. Among their best-selling products are The Animal, Ants in the Pants, Guesstures, Brain Warp, California Roller Baby, Real Talking Bubba, Masterpiece, My Size Barbie, Casey Cartwheel, Jennie Gymnast, and Hot Wheels Criss Cross Crash.

Christiansen, Ole Kirk (1891-1958): A Danish toy maker, Christiansen began making wooden toys before he started Lego, the "automatic binding brick," in 1946.

Coords, Henry H. (1915-1995): Coords led Fisher-Price, served as TMA president, and championed safety standards as in his own company's virtually indestructible preschool toys.

Cowen, Joshua Lionel (1887-1965): A leader of the electric toy industry, a pioneer developer and inventor, his Lionel trains set the pace for the industry. Cowen and his business partner Harry Grant in 1901 introduced their version of an electric train with a dry cell battery connected directly to the rails in New York City's Ingersoll department store as a window display. Personal orders allowed the company to consolidate in 1902 and introduce the catalogs and advertisements that have become classics among collectors. Although Lionel toy electric trains were not the first, they were the most successful (the American Flyer line taken over by A. C. Gilbert being its greatest rival) and survived the Great Depression. A little handcar featuring Mickey and Minnie Mouse in 1934 at the crank may have saved the company from bankruptcy. Marketing to fathers and sons as a family activity was its hallmark.

Disney, Walt (1901-1966): A legend and folk hero with a fertile imagination, Disney's animated characters Mickey Mouse, Donald Duck, Goofy, and others, beginning in the late 1920s, lent themselves to innumerable toy creations. His 1950s *Mickey Mouse Club* hosted the first national commercial by a toy manufacturer, Mattel, a company thereafter long associated with Disney. Disney himself was noted for his joy, optimism, and playful spirit.

Fisher, Homer G. (1898-1975): Fisher founded Fisher-Price and served as its president and chairman from its beginning in 1930 until 1969. His company was the largest and most respected manufacturer of preschool toys. All had to show "intrinsic play value, ingenuity, strong construction, good value for the money, and action features." As head of TMA in 1938, Fisher helped to establish its statistical committee.

Fryer, Jerome O. (1918-1983): As president of CBS Toys, Fryer in 1950 acquired S. Gabriel Sons, Inc. His company later included Hubley, Gilbert, and Ideal.

Gilbert, A. C. [Alfred Carlton] (1884-1961): A Yale-trained physician and Olympic pole vaulter, Gilbert first produced magician supplies with his

Mysto Co., then turned out erector sets and chemistry kits with his eponymous company in New Haven, Connecticut. Although Gilbert thought of the idea of erector kits in the fall of 1911 while passing under steel girders on the commuter train from Connecticut to New York, there were competing manufacturers of similar products. In 1918, he acquired the U.S. patent for steel-beamed construction sets from the Structo Manufacturing Co. of Freeport, Illinois (the British rights went to Meccano). He later purchased the American Flyer toy train company. With an inventive mind and business acumen, Gilbert early proposed spreading toy sales evenly throughout the year. He helped to establish the Toy Manufacturers of America in 1916 and served as its first president. During World War I he convinced the U.S. government to keep the Christmas gift-giving tradition alive. A. C. Gilbert's Discovery Village in his hometown of Salem, Oregon, strives to further many of his values such as provoking curiosity, fostering enjoyment, and enabling understanding in youth.

Glass, Marvin (1914-1974): One of the world's foremost toy designers, Glass founded Marvin Glass and Associates in 1941 where many professionals operated. His products included Mr. Machine, Mousetrap, Kissy Doll, and Rock 'em Sock 'em Robots.

Greenman, Nathan (1916-1976): A foremost toy wholesaler, Greenman was a major force behind Greenman Brothers, Inc., one of the largest toy wholesalers in the United States.

Grey, Richard E. (1934-): In 1958, Dick Grey joined Milt Grey, Inc., his father's marketing firm, when it had Tyco as a client (and when it was mostly a model train manufacturer.) He was president of Tyco in 1973 and chairman of the board in 1991. Grey led the company through aggressive growth and marketing. By 1992, Tyco was America's third largest toy company with toy cars, Matchbox cars, preschool toys, and games among its products. In 1997 Mattel took over Tyco and continued to market toys using its name.

Handler, Ruth (1917-2002) and Handler, Elliott: "First couple" of the toy industry, the Handlers developed Barbie in 1959 after the Swiss doll Lilli and named it after their daughter. They named Ken after their son. Their company Mattel (a name created out of an amalgam from Elliott and Mattson, an early partner) was the first to advertise nationally on television (on Disney's *Mickey Mouse Club* in 1955). In the early twenty-first century Hasbro and Mattel, from which the Handlers had long been separated, continued to change places as the first and second toy manufacturers in the United States.

Hassenfeld, Alan G. (1948-): As current chairman and CEO of Hasbro, Inc., Hassenfeld diversified the company, expanded international operations, and furthered corporate responsibility.

Hassenfeld, Merrill L. (1918-1979): Hassenfeld took the family business of Hassenfeld Brothers begun by his father and two uncles and transformed it from a school supply company to a toy industry during World War II, beginning with doctor and nurse kits and air-raid warden sets. He was company president from 1943 to 1974. Among his products were the classics Mr. Potato Head and G.I. Joe.

Hassenfeld, Stephen D. (1942-1989): Architect of Hasbro as a modern toy company, Stephen Hassenfeld left it, through acquisitions of companies such as Milton Bradley and Tonka, as the world's largest in 1989 (closely followed by Mattel). He established the Hasbro Children's Foundation and the Hasbro Charitable Trust.

Henson, Jim (1936-1990): Muppet creator, Henson emphasized the themes of love and friendship and set them to music. His *Sesame Street* television program on PBS and films led to toys and games based on characters such as Kermit the Frog, Miss Piggy, Big Bird, Bert and Ernie, the Cookie Monster, and Oscar the Grouch.

Kalinske, Thomas J. (1944-): In the toy industry since 1972, Kalinske helped build successful brands and companies. He was president of Mattel, Universal Matchbox, and Sega of America. Kalinske helped to establish an industry-wide video game rating system.

Kasch, Morey W. (1907-1972): A wholesaler with H. W. Kasch, Co., Kasch emphasized speedy deliveries and customer service.

Lazarus, Charles (1923-): Lazarus pioneered one-stop shopping for children's toys with Toys "R" Us patterned after self-service supermarkets. He believed in selling brand names for less by sheer volume and huge selections.

Loomis, Bernard (1923-): An expert toy marketer who worked as vice president of Kenner, group vice president of General Mills, partner with Hasbro, and consultant to Tyco.

Marx, Louis (1896-1982): Nicknamed "the toy king of America" and "the Henry Ford of the toy industry," Marx established the Louis Marx Toy Co. in 1921. He received his start with Ferdinand Strauss, the "toy king" until the 1920s, when his firm failed. Marx was noted for making less expensive versions of already popular toys rather than for his innovative designs. Because he sold quite profitably through mail-order catalogs and department stores, he was a latecomer to advertising on television. But by 1950, his toy company was the world's largest. He offered quality at the lowest possible price. By the 1960s his company's logo of Magic Marxie was featured on television. Marx was the first to mass produce mechanical toys in the United States. His company did not long outlive him, however.

Michtom, Benjamin F. (1901-1980): One of the best promoters of toys ever, Michtom made the Ideal Toy and Novelty Co. founded by his father Morris (d. 1938) a hit. He was one of the first to use licensed products, among them character dolls such as those of film personalities Shirley Temple, Deanna Durbin, Fanny Brice, Charlie McCarthy, and Judy Garland. His Toni home permanent doll was an example of "a product within a product." In 1953, Benjamin Michtom secured a license for the U.S. Forest Service to make Smokey Bear dolls.

Moore, Howard (1930-): As a merchandiser with Toys "R" Us, Moore focused on strategic line planning and product selection.

Parker, Edward P. (1912-1974): Chairman of Parker Brothers in the 1970s who sprang to the defense of the board game Monopoly when Atlantic City proposed renaming Baltic and Mediterranean Avenues.

Parker, George S. (1866-1952): Legendary founder of Parker Brothers game company, the youngest of three who later brought his brothers into the company. Parker was known for emphasizing games that accentuated the fun of making money rather than teaching moral lessons. Among the most famous on his watch were mah-jongg (a Chinese import) and Monopoly. Parker Brothers games are currently sold by Hasbro.

Pressman, Jack C. (1890-1959): Founded J. Pressman and Co. in 1922 (later Pressman Toy Co.) in partnership with Max Eibetz. When he split up with Eibetz in 1947, Pressman's wife Lynn took over his former partner's role which was overseeing the company rather than handling sales. After his death, Pressman's sons Edward and James also helped out.

Among Pressman's firsts was the introduction of Chinese checkers into the United States in 1928. In 1938 the company produced Wordy, based on a prototype of Scrabble but using colored tiles. It was the first to produce children's barber sets, a beauty kit in a hat box, and a dentist set. The company is known for marketing generic games such as chess, checkers, pick-up-sticks, and tiddledywinks. In 2000, Pressman was the third largest U.S. game manufacturer.

Raizen, Charles S. (1892-1967): As a summer employee of a company that manufactured tissue embroidery patterns which could be transferred to cloth using heat, Raizen invented a fun way to transfer patterns using friction. In 1917, Raizen bought out his boss and took over the company, changing the name from the Friction Transfer Pattern Company to Transogram. Raizen established the Toy Research Institute, one of the first toy designers' think tanks. As early as the 1920s he tested his toys with a child psychologist, a fact he used to market his products. He introduced items during the 1930s such as The Little Country Doctor and Nurse Kit and Trik Trak cars. Raizen was president of TMA in 1960.

Under Raizen, Transogram was a major player in the 1950s and 1960s, especially scoring with *Dragnet* in 1955 and later with Play Your Hunch, Tic Tac Dough, and Truth or Consequences. Raizen's company was sold two years after his death and did not long survive him.

Schoenhut, Albert (1849-1912): Born into a toy-making family in Germany, Albert Schoenhut immigrated to Philadelphia in 1866. By the time of his death, he was not only the largest American toy maker but also was the first in the United States to export toys to Germany. Fame originally came to him for introducing a toy piano in 1872, but later he became known for wooden and circus-themed toys. In 1935, Schoenhut's company went out of business because of the Great Depression. Otto Schoenhut, Albert's son, started a new toy company named O. Schoenhut in 1936, thereby carrying on the family legacy.

Schwarz, Frederick (F. A. O.): Frederick August Otto Schwarz was one of four brothers from Germany to set up American toy stores. Henry's was in Baltimore, Richard's in Boston, Gustav's in Philadelphia, and Frederick's in New York. Only the last still remains.

Schwarz, Larry: In 1997 he created Rumpus Toys, a privately owned, Internet-driven toy company. It features items such as Gus Gutz, whose organs can be pulled out of its mouth and the Rumpus Road Rocket, a big toy school bus painted white with bright polka dots.

Shea, James J. (1889-1977): Shea rescued Milton Bradley Co. in the 1930s and headed it for over thirty years. He was a philanthropist and a believer in corporate responsibility.

Steiner, Albert (1895-1977): Steiner headed Kenner Products Co. and led a family business team that included two brothers and his son. His company became famous for child versions of adult activities, such as the Easy-Bake Oven and Give a Show Projector.

Wagner, Raymond P. (1932-1985): After retail experience with Sears, Wagner was Mattel's president from 1973 to 1983. TMA chairman in 1981, Wagner was known for being able to visualize toys through the eyes of children.

Wenkstern, Russell L. (1912-2000): President and CEO of Tonka from 1952 to 1974, Wenkstern turned that company into a success. Under his auspices, Tonka trucks were known for their safety and durability.

Ziv, Sy (1925-): In a twenty-six-year career at Toys "R" Us, Ziv promoted the toy business and helped many small toy manufacturing companies stay in business.

Bibliography

Books

Anderson, Brian, Iona Opie, and Robert Opie. *The Treasures of Childhood.* New York: Arcade Publishing, 1989.

Arnold, Karen South. *Playing Grandma's Games.* Ouray, CO: Western Reflections Publishing Company, 2000.

Auerbach, Stevanne. *F.A.O. Schwarz: Toys for a Lifetime. Enhancing Childhood Through Play.* New York: Universe Publications, 1999.

Barenholtz, Bernard and Inez McClintock. *American Antique Toys, 1830-1900.* New York: Harry N. Abrams, 1980.

Bartlett, Vernon. *The Past of Pastimes.* Hamden, CT: Archon Books, 1969.

Baxter, George H. and Russell A. Stultz. *Magic Cards Simplified: For Player Parents and Beginning Players of Magic: The Gathering.* Plano, TX: Wordware Publishing, 1997.

Bell, R.C. *Board and Card Games from Many Civilizations.* New York: Dover Publications, 1979.

Bird, William L. Jr. *Paint by Number.* Washington, DC: Smithsonian Institution, National Museum of American History in association with Princeton Architectural Press, 2001.

Bloemker, Larry, Robert Genat, and Ed Weirick. *Pedal Cars.* Osceola, WI: MBI, 1999.

Botermans, Jack, Tony Burrett, Peter van Deift, and Carla van Splunteren. *The World of Games.* New York: Facts on File, Inc., 1989.

Buchholz, Shirley. *A Century of Celluloid Dolls.* Cumberland, MD: Hobby House Press, 1983.

Collector's Value Guide: Pokemon, Secondary Market Price Guide and Collector Handbook. Middletown, CT: Checkerbee Publishing, 1999.

Cooper, Patty and Dian Ziliner. *Toy Buildings. 1880-1980.* Atglen, PA: Schiffer Publishing, 2000.

Costello, Matthew J. *The Greatest Games of All Time.* New York: John Wiley & Sons, 1991.

Cross, Gary. *Kids' Stuff: Toys and the Changing World of American Childhood.* Cambridge: Harvard University Press, 1997.

Dennis, Lee. *Antique American Games, 1840-1940.* Elkins Park, PA: Warman Publishing Co., 1986.

Diagram Group. *The Way to Play*. New York: Paddington Press, 1975, and Bantam Books, 1977.

Diagram Visual Information Ltd. *Rules of the Game: Board and Tile Games*. New York: Paddington Press, 1974, and Crown Publishers, 1977.

DiNoto, Andrea, ed. *The Encyclopedia of Collectibles*. Alexandria, VA: Time-Life Books, 1978.

Dolan, Maryanne. *The World of Dolls*. Iola, WI: Krause Publication, 1998.

Finnegan, Stephanie and Walter Pfeiffer. Madame Alexander Dolls: An American Legend. 1999.

Fleming, Dan. *Powerplay: Toys As Popular Culture*. New York: Manchester University Press, 1996.

Flick, Pauline. *Discovering Toys and Toy Museums*. Tring, England: Shire Publishing, 1971.

Fraser, Antonia. *A History of Toys*. London, New York: Spring Books, 1966.

Frederick, Filis. *Design and Sell Toys, Games, and Crafts*. Radnor, PA: Chilton Book Co., 1977.

Gardiner, Gordon and Alistair Morris. *The Illustrated Encyclopedia of Metal Toys*. New York: Harmony Books, 1984.

Gelber, Steven M. *Hobbies: Leisure and the Culture of Work in America*. New York: Columbia University Press, 1999.

Gerken, Jo Elizabeth. *Wonderful Dolls of Papier Mache*. Lincoln, NE: Union College Press, 1970.

Gibson, Walter. *Family Games America Plays*. Garden City, NY: Doubleday, 1970.

Gilbert, A. C. with Marshall McClintock. *The Man Who Lives in Paradise*. New York: Rinehart and Company, 1954.

Gorden, Lesley. *Peepshow into Paradise: A History of Children's Toys*. London: Harrap, 1953.

Green, Joey. *The Official Slinky Book*. New York: Berkeley Publishing Group, 1999.

Grunfeld, Frederic. *Games of the World*. New York: Plenary Publications International, 1975.

Hake, Ted. *Hake's Guide to Comic Character Collectibles: An Illustrated Price Guide to 100 Years of Comic Strip Characters*. Radnor, PA: Wallace-Homestead Book Company, 1993.

————. Hakes' Guide to TV Collectibles. Radnor, PA: Wallace-Homestead Book Company, 1990.

Handler, Elliot. *The Impossible Really Is Possible: The Story of Mattel*. New York: Newcomen Society in North America, 1968.

Harry, Lou. *It's Slinky! The Fun and Wonderful Toy*. Philadelphia: Running Press, 2000.

Hart, Clive. *Kites: An Historical Survey,* Third Edition. Mount Vernon, NY: Paul P. Appel, 1982.

Heaton, Tom. *The Encyclopedia of Harx Action Figures: A Price and Identification Guide.* Iola, WI: Krause Publications, 1999.

Herlocker, Dawn. *Antique Trader's Doll Makers and Marks: A Guide to Identification.* 1999. Norfolk, VA: Antique Trader Books.

Herron, R. Lane. *Warman's Dolls: A Value and Identification Guide.* Iola, WI: Krause Publications, 1998.

Hertz, Louis H. *The Toy Collector.* New York: Funk & Wagnalls, 1969.

Hillier, Mary. *Pageant of Toys.* New York: Toplinger Publishing Company, 1966.

Hoffman, David. *Kid Stuff: Great Toys from Our Childhood.* San Francisco: Chronicle Books, 1990.

Hollander, Ron. *All Aboard!: The Story of Joshua Lionel Cowen and His Lionel Train Company,* Revised Edition. New York: Workman Publications, 2000.

Horowitz, Roger, ed. *Boys and Their Toys? Masculinity, Class, and Technology in America.* New York: Routledge, 2001.

Huizinga, Johan. *Homo Ludens: A Study of the Play Element in Culture.* London: Temple Smith, 1970 [1938].

Hunter, Tim. *Bobbing Head Dolls. 1960-2000.* Iola, WI: Krause Publications, 2000.

Jackson, Emily. *Toys of Other Days.* New York: B. Blom, 1968 [1908].

Johnson, Stancil E.D. *Frisbee: A Practitioner's Manual and Definitive Treatise.* New York: Workman Publishers, 1975.

Ketchum, William C. *Toys and Games.* New York: Cooper-Hewitt Museum, 1981.

King, Constance. *The Century of the Teddy Bear.* Woodbridge, England: Antique Collectors' Club, 1997.

———. *The Encyclopedia of Toys.* New York: Crown Books, 1978.

Liljeblod, Cynthia Boris. *TV Toys and the Shows That Inspired Them.* Iola, WI: Krause Publications, 1996.

Lindenberger, Jan with Judy D. Morris. *Encyclopedia of Cabbage Patch Kids: The 1980s.* Atglen, PA: Schiffer Publications, 1999.

Lord, H.G. *Forever Barbie: The Unauthorized Biography of a Real Doll.* New York: Morrow and Co., 1994.

Love, Brian. *Great Board Games.* New York: Macmillan, 1979.

Luke, Tim. *American Insider's Guide to Toys and Games.* London: Octopus Publishing Group, 2002.

Malloy, Alex G. *American Games: Comprehensive Collector's Guide Featuring the Alex G. Malloy Game Collection.* Iola, WI: Krause Publications, 2000.

Massucci, Edoardo. *Cars for Kids.* New York: Rizzoli International, 1983.

McClintock, Inez. *Toys in America.* Washington, DC: Public Affairs Press, 1961.

McClinton, Katharine Morrison. *Antiques of American Childhood.* New York: Clarkson N. Potter, 1970.

McDonough, Yona Zeldis, ed. *The Barbie Chronicles: A Living Doll Turns Forty.* New York: Simon and Schuster, 1999.

McNulty, Lyndi Steward. *Wallace-Homestead Price Guide to Plastic Collectibles.* Greensboro, NC: Wallace-Homestead Book Company, 1992.

Meisenheimer, Lucky. *Lucky's Collectors Guide to 20th Century Yo-Yos: The History and Values.* Orlando, FL: Lucky J's Swim and Surf, Inc., 1999.

Mellilo, Marcie. *The Ultimate Barbie Doll Book.* Iola, WI: Krause Publications, 1996.

Miller, G. Wayne. *Toy Wars: The Epic Struggle Between G.I. Joe, Barbie, and the Companies That Make Them.* New York: Random House, 1998.

Murry, Harold J. *History of Board Games Other Than Chess.* New York: Greenberg Publishers, Inc., 1940.

O'Brien, Richard. *The Story of American Toys.* New York: Abbeville Press, 1990.

Opie, Iona Archibald. *The Treasures of Childhood: Books, Toys, and Games from the Opie Collection.* New York: Arcade Publishing, 1989.

Orbanes, Philip. *The Game Makers: The Story of Parker Brothers from Tiddlely Winks to Trivial Pursuit.* Boston: Harvard Business School Press, 2004.

Orbanes, Philip. *The Monopoly Companion.* Boston: Bob Adams, Inc., 1988.

Parker Brothers, Inc. *90 Years of Fun: 1883-1973—The History of Parker Brothers.* Salem, MA: Parker Brothers, 1973.

———. *75 Years of Fun: The Story of Parker Brothers, Inc.* Salem, MA: Parker Brothers, 1958.

Pelham, David. *The Penguin Book of Kites.* New York: Penguin Books, 1976.

Pennell, Paul. *Children's Cars.* Buckinghamshire, UK: Shire Publications, Ltd., 1986.

Piggott, John and Richard Sharp. *The Book of Games.* New York: Galahad Books, 1977.

Polizzi, Rick. *Baby Boomer Games: Identification and Value Guide.* Paducah, KY: Collector Books, 1995.

Polizzi, Rick and Fred Schaefer. *Spin Again: Board Games from the Fifties and Sixties.* San Francisco: Chronicle Books, 1991.

Reed, Robert. *Bears and Dolls in Advertising: Guide to Collectible Characters and Critters.* Iola, WI: Krause Publications, 1998.

Rich, Mark. *100 Greatest Baby Boomer Toys.* Iola, WI: Krause Publications, 2000.

———. *Toys A to Z: A Guide and Dictionary for Collectors, Antique Dealers, and Enthusiasts.* Iola, WI: Krause Publications, 2002.

Rinker, Harry L. *Collector's Guide to Toys, Games, and Puzzles.* Radnor, PA: Wallace-Homestead Book Company, 1991.

Rinker, Harry L. *Rinker on Collectibles.* Radnor, PA: Wallace-Homestead Book Company, 1989.

Rushlow, Bonnie B. *A Century of Crayola Collectibles.* Grantersville, MD: Hobby House Press, 2003.

Santelmo, Vincent. *The Complete Encyclopedia to G.I. Joe,* Third Edition. Iola, WI: Krause Publications, 2001.

Schoonmaker, Patricia. *A Collector's History of the Teddy Bear.* Cumberland, MD: Hobby House Press, 1981.

————. *Patsy Doll Family Encyclopedia.* Cumberland, MD: Hobby House Press, 1992.

Schroeder, Joseph J., compiler. *The Wonderful World of Toys, Games and Dolls. 1860-1930.* Northfield, IL: Digest Books, 1971.

Schwarz, Marvin. *F.A.O. Schwarz Toys Through the Years.* Garden City, NY: Doubleday, 1975.

Shea, James Jr. (as told to Charles Mercer). *It's All in the Game.* New York: G.P. Putnam, 1960.

————. *The Milton Bradley Story.* New York: The Newcomen Society in North America, 1973.

Slocum, Jerry and Jack Botermans. *Puzzles Old and New: How to Make and Solve Them.* Seattle: University of Washington Press, 1987.

Stephan, Elizabeth A., ed. *Ultimate Price Guide to Fast Food Collectibles.* Iola, WI: Krause Publications, 1999.

Stern, Sydney and Ted Schoenhaus. *Toyland: The High-Stakes Game of the Toy Industry.* Chicago: Contemporary Books, 1990.

Stevens, Beth. *Billions of Balls: Historical Toys.* Logan, IA: Perfection Learning, 1999.

Sutton-Smith, Brian. *Toys As Culture.* New York: Gardner Press, 1986.

Tosa, Marco. *Barbie: Four Decades of Fashion, Fantasy, and Fun,* translated from Italian by Linda M. Esklund. New York: H.N. Abrams, 1998.

Toys and Games. Alexandria, VA: Time-Life Books, 1991.

Varaste, Christopher. *Face of the American Dream: Barbie Doll, 1959-1971.* Grantsville, MD: Hobby House Press, 1999.

White, Gwen. *Antique Toys and Their Background.* New York: Arco, 1971.

White, Larry. *Cracker Jack Toys: The Unauthorized Guide.* Atglen, PA: Schiffer Publications, 1997.

Whitehill, Bruce. *Games: American Boxed Games and Their Makers, 1822-1992.* Radnor, PA: Wallace-Homestead Book Company, 1992.

Whitehouse, Francis. *Table Games of Georgian and Victorian Days.* London: P. Garnett, 1951.

Whitton, Blair. *Toys.* New York: Alfred A. Knopf, 1984.

Williams, Anne D. *Jigsaw Puzzles: An Illustrated History and Price Guide.* Radnor, PA: Wallace-Homestead Book Company, 1990.

Wojahn, Ellen. *Playing by Different Rules.* New York: Amacon, 1988.

Wood, Clement and Gloria Goddard, eds. *The Complete Book of Games.* Garden City, NY: Doubleday and Co., 1940.

Wulffson, Don. *Toys! Amazing Stories Behind Some Great Inventions.* New York: Henry Holt, 2000.

Articles

Augustyn, Frederick J. Jr. "The American Switzerland: New England As a Toy-Making Center." *Journal of Popular Culture* (Summer 2002): 1-13.

Bidwell, Carol. "Creating a Game of Family Conversation." *The Washington Times,* January 26, 1999, p. E4.

"Birth of a Bear." *The Washington Times,* January 26, 2003, p. A2.

Broad, William J. "Rocket Science, Served Up Soggy." *The New York Times,* July 31, 2001, p. Fl.

Cook, Chris. "The Yo-Yo Vault. Part I: The Toys That Made Noyz" [*sic*]. *Yo-Yo World Magazine* (September/October 1999): 112-115.

Crockett, Stephen A. "Outside the Lines at the Crayola Store: Local Colors—and Freebies—Draw a Crowd of Parents." *The Washington Post,* June 22, 2002, p. Cl.

Dianis, Charles. "Raggedy Ann Inducted into Toy Hall of Fame; Lovable Red-Haired Doll Was Created in Norwalk." *The Stamford Advocate,* March 28, 2002.

Folkers, Richard. "Your Kids Will Speak Furbish." *U.S. News and World Report,* October 12, 1998, p. 73.

"Get Smart: Mixing Trivia, Mime, and Even Sculpting, A Game Named Cranium Gives Brain Strain to Fans Like Julia Roberts." *People Weekly,* May 22, 2000, p. 180.

Gordon, John Steele. "The Monopoly Nobody Doesn't Like: The Game That Has Sold 200 Million Sets Was Born to Teach Its Players About the Evils of Capitalism." *American Heritage* (September 2000): 15-16.

Hamilton, Martha McNeil. "A Timely Toy to the Rescue: One Action Figure Stands Tall in Newly Complicated Kids' Market." *The Washington Post,* October 3, 2001, p. El.

Hunker, Paula Gray. "Toys Are a Plus if Playtime Is Balanced." *The Washington Times,* November 30, 1999, p. El.

Lewinson, Ann. "Possessed by Pokémon: End-of-the Millennium Decadence Rears Its Adorably Monstrous Head." *The Fairfield* [Connecticut] *County Weekly,* December 23, 1999, pp. 15-16.

Leyden, Liz. "At Age 40, Barbie Gets Career Advice: Mattel, Girls Inc. Team Up on Make-Over Ideas." *The Washington Post,* March 27, 1999, p. El.

McKenna, Dave. "Slipped Disc." *Washington City Paper,* August 10, 2001, p. 16.

McLloyd, Vonnie C. "Verbal Interaction in Social Play: Mixed-Age Preschool Dyads." *Journal of Black Studies* (June 1979): 469-488.

Mergen, Bernard. "The Discovery of Children's Play." *American Quarterly* (October 1975): 399-420.

"'Millionaire,' 'Simpsons' Win the Board Game." *USA Today,* October 15, 2000, p. 15E.

"No Java: Starbucks Brings Out Another Board Game." *USA Today,* June 14, 2002, p. Dl.

"Norwalk Museum's New Curator Promotes Legend of Raggedy Ann." *The Stamford Advocate,* November 17, 2000.

Oldenburg, Don. "The Top Toys? The Lists Are Endless." *The Washington Post,* December 14, 1999, p. C4.

"One Less Babe in Toyland." *Newsweek,* March 25, 2002, p. 9.

"Our Favorite Playthings." *Time,* December 9, 1996, pp. 76-77.

"Privates' Parts: When Elderly G.I. Joes Begin to Lose Their Hair War, Craig Blankenship Provides Coif Medicine." *People Weekly,* January 24, 2000, p. 93.

Puig, Claudia. "Toying with Collecting: Preserve Items or Play with Them? That's the Story Behind 'Story 2.'" *USA Today,* November 23, 1999, p. Dl.

Py-Liberman, Beth. "The Colors of Childhood: Crayola Crayons Take Us All Back with Their Fondly Remembered Look, Scent, and Feel on Paper." *Smithsonian* (November 1999): 32-36.

Schwartzman, Helen B. "The Anthropological Study of Children's Play." *Annual Review of Anthropology* (1976): 289-328.

Solomon, Michael. "The 50 Greatest Game Shows of All Time." *TV Guide,* January 27, 2001, pp. 22-41.

"Spring to Life: Bobblehead Dolls Become Big Business." *The Washington Post,* June 5, 2002, p. C16.

Stearns, Peter N. "Girls, Boys, and Emotions: Redefinitions and Historical Change." *Journal of American History* (June 1993): 36-74.

Streitfeld, Lisa. "The Circle at Play." *The Stamford Advocate,* December 27, 1998, p. Dl.

Szadkowski, Joseph and Jacquie Kubin. "Good Bets for Any Santa's Sack." *The Washington Times,* November 25, 1998, p. FlO.

Veigle, Anne. "Dolls' House Displays Tiny, Dazzling World." *The Washington Times,* March 16, 1999, p. E7.

Watson, Bruce. "'Hello, Boys! Become an Erector Master Engineer!'" *Smithsonian* (May 1999): 120-134.

"Where Are They Now? Cabbage Patch Kids." *Time,* December 9, 1996, p. 25.

Wilkinson, Doris Yvonne. "Racial Socialization Through Children's Toys: A Sociohistorical Examination." *Journal of Black Studies* (September 1974): 96-109.

Wilson, Craig. "Lionel: On Track for Another Century." *USA Today,* December 15, 2000, p. Dl.

"With Toys Like This, Who Needs Friends?" *Newsweek,* November 13, 2000, p. 14.

Woulfe, Molly. "Toying with Tastelessness: Top 10 Stocking Stinkers Bring No Joy to the World." *The Washington Times,* December 16, 1999, p. B8.

Zoroya, Gregg. "Block Party: Legoland California Builds Adventure for the Young at Heart." *USA Today,* March 19, 1999, p. Dl.

Periodicals

AGPC Quarterly (Marlborough, MA: The Association of Game and Puzzle Collectors).

Baby Boomer Collectibles (Dubuque, IA: Antique Trader Publications).

Beckett Pokemon Collector (Dallas, TX: Beckett Publications).

Betty's Attic: Where Memories of Yesterday Live on Today (Bradenton, FL).

Bits and Pieces: The Source for Clever Puzzles and Intriguing Gifts (Stevens Point, WI).

Collecting Toys (Waukesha, WI: Kalmbach Publishing).

Contemporary Doll Collector (Livonia, MI: Scott Publications, 1994-).

Model and Toy Collector (Akron, OH: Toy Scouts, Inc.).

Reminisce: The Magazine That Brings Back the Good Times (Greendale, WI: Reiman Publications).

The Teddy Bears and Friends (Cumberland, MD: Hobby House Press, 1983-).

Toy Collector and Price Guide (Iola, WI: Krause Publications, 1993-).

Toy Shop Annual 2000 (Iola, WI: Krause Publications, 2000).

Toy Trader (Waupaca, WI: Antique Trader Publications).

Calendars

Toy Shop's Favorite Advertising Icon Toys! 2003 Calendar (Iola, WI: Krause Publications, 2002).

Toys We Remember 2003 Calendar (San Rafael, CA: Cedco Publishing Company, 2002).

Exhibits and Symposia

"The Art of the Puzzle, Astounding and Confounding," Exhibit at Katonah (New York) Museum of Art, October 15, 2000-January 7, 2001.

"Pedal to the Metal: A History of Children's Pedal Cars," Exhibit at The Stamford (Connecticut) Museum and Nature Center, September 14, 2003-January 4, 2004.

"The Playful Mind: A Symposium at the National Museum of American History," Washington, DC, September 22-23, 2000.

"Shadows and Strings: Puppetry Around the Globe," Exhibit at The Bruce Museum, Greenwich, December 6, 2003-February 29, 2004.

"Spinning Spheres and Whirling Wheels: The Art of Play," Exhibit at The Bruce Museum, Greenwich, CT, November 1998-January 1999.

"Toying with Architecture: The Building Toy in the Arena of Play, 1800 to the Present," Exhibit at Katonah (New York) Museum of Art, September 28, 1997-January 4, 1998.

"200 Years of Toys and Games—Philadelphia: A Center of Manufacturing and Marketing," Ongoing Exhibit at the Atwater Kent Museum, Philadelphia, Pennsylvania.

Television Collectors' Programs

The Incurable Collector (A&E).

Personal Effects: The Collectibles Show (FOX).

Treasures in Your Home: The World of Collecting (PAX).

SPECIAL 25%-OFF DISCOUNT!

Order a copy of this book with this form or online at:

http://www.haworthpress.com/store/product.asp?sku=5051

DICTIONARY OF TOYS AND GAMES IN AMERICAN POPULAR CULTURE

_____ in hardbound at $22.46 (regularly $29.95) (ISBN: 0-7890-1503-X)

_____ in softbound at $11.21 (regularly $14.95) (ISBN: 0-7890-1504-8)

Or order online and use special offer code HEC25 in the shopping cart.

COST OF BOOKS_____

OUTSIDE US/CANADA/
MEXICO: ADD 20%_____

POSTAGE & HANDLING_____
*(US: $5.00 for first book & $2.00
for each additional book)*
*(Outside US: $6.00 for first book
& $2.00 for each additional book)*

SUBTOTAL_____

IN CANADA: ADD 7% GST_____

STATE TAX_____
*(NY, OH, MN, CA, IN, & SD residents,
add appropriate local sales tax)*

FINAL TOTAL_____
*(If paying in Canadian funds,
convert using the current
exchange rate, UNESCO
coupons welcome)*

☐ **BILL ME LATER:** ($5 service charge will be added)
(Bill-me option is good on US/Canada/Mexico orders only;
not good to jobbers, wholesalers, or subscription agencies.)

☐ Check here if billing address is different from
shipping address and attach purchase order and
billing address information.

Signature_____

☐ **PAYMENT ENCLOSED: $_____**

☐ **PLEASE CHARGE TO MY CREDIT CARD.**

☐ Visa ☐ MasterCard ☐ AmEx ☐ Discover
☐ Diner's Club ☐ Eurocard ☐ JCB

Account # _____

Exp. Date_____

Signature_____

Prices in US dollars and subject to change without notice.

NAME_____

INSTITUTION_____

ADDRESS_____

CITY_____

STATE/ZIP_____

COUNTRY_____ COUNTY (NY residents only)_____

TEL_____ FAX_____

E-MAIL_____

May we use your e-mail address for confirmations and other types of information? ☐ Yes ☐ No
We appreciate receiving your e-mail address and fax number. Haworth would like to e-mail or fax special
discount offers to you, as a preferred customer. **We will never share, rent, or exchange your e-mail address
or fax number.** We regard such actions as an invasion of your privacy.

Order From Your Local Bookstore or Directly From
The Haworth Press, Inc.
10 Alice Street, Binghamton, New York 13904-1580 • USA
TELEPHONE: 1-800-HAWORTH (1-800-429-6784) / Outside US/Canada: (607) 722-5857
FAX: 1-800-895-0582 / Outside US/Canada: (607) 771-0012
E-mailto: orders@haworthpress.com
PLEASE PHOTOCOPY THIS FORM FOR YOUR PERSONAL USE.
http://www.HaworthPress.com

BOF03